Kathryn,
Walk with love
and beauty!
love Heron

Grandmothers
of the Wind

Menopause, Wisdom,
and Power

Linda Heron Wind

Heron Press
Rochester, New York

D1221456

Cover art and illustrations by Sandra R. Gifford

ISBN 1-890027-00-6

Library of Congress Catalogue Number: 96-095224

Contents

Acknowledgements

I thank the Grandmothers for calling me to do this work and for their continued support and Wisdom.

Without the gifts and encouragement of my sister and friend Annette Margaret, this book would never have come into being. Thank you, Annette, for remembering my heart song when I forgot and for singing it back to me!

I am grateful to all my wonderful friends and family who call forth my best self with their love.

A special thanks to my editor for her eagle eye and attention to detail; to Sandy Gifford for the beauty she brings forth through her art work in the illustrations and on the cover; and to Judy Natal for the gift of my photo on the back cover.

I thank the Grandmothers of the Grandmother Lodge for their courage to walk as women of power and for helping my vision become manifest.

Dedication

This book is dedicated to women all over the Earth who are hearing the call of the Wisdom Teachings. May we dance through this initiation into the Wise Woman years with the power of our own Knowing.

Introduction

Until I wrote my first book, *New Moon Rising*, I never understood where books came from. I guess I thought it was from the author's mind. When *New Moon Rising* was done, however, my heart knew better.

So, when the Grandmothers called me to write this second book, I was well aware of the journey that it would entail, and that when it was finished, I would be different. It does not feel as though I wrote this book, but rather that the book has written me.

Grandmothers of the Wind is my gift, a teaching, a call to my sisters to find the universal Wisdom that lives within. It is a challenge to bring that Wisdom forth and make of it an offering to a world hungry for Truth.

The Grandmothers

My interest in menopause was kindled by the increasing number of physical changes in my body as I made my approach toward the age of fifty. I read everything I could find on the subject, from medical approaches to accounts of individual women who had gone through "the change." Nothing I read seemed to satisfy me. The feeling persisted that there was a missing piece. There *had* to be more.

But what was it that I was looking for? I wasn't exactly sure, but one thing I knew was that I wanted to move into and through my own menopause in an empowered way and emerge into the next phase of my life with joy and beauty. I wanted to find out how best to do this.

In gathering material for my earlier book, *New Moon Rising,* which focuses on menstruation and its relationship to the power of the feminine, I had come across suggestions that menopause, like menstruation, was related to women's wisdom and power. I had participated in several Grandmother Lodge inductions in which women of menopausal age shared their wisdom with younger women and made vows to nurture all the children in the circle of life. Yet none of what I read or learned told me *what* this wisdom was or *how* one became wise. This body of wisdom was obviously considered to be of great value and was so highly prized that many cultures around the world had ritualized its sharing with ceremonies and induction rites.

I felt as though there ought to be a course of study or some sort of wholistic preparation that could serve as a guide during the years women are shifting their primary focus from motherhood and careers to . . . what? I thought that perhaps the information I was looking for had been lost long ago, buried with the remains of the broken goddess figures of matrifocal times.

In the midst of my searching, I began to think that I might write something about the subject. I don't know how or when this idea planted itself within my mind, but there it was. Could I find out more about the connection between menopause and women's wisdom and power? I didn't have any specific ideas on how I would go about doing this, and I really didn't spend much time thinking about it.

About this time, I met with a close friend of mine, Annette Margaret. (Annette is a visionary, and it was through her that I had been introduced to the spirit grandmother who helped me write *New Moon Rising*.) She asked me if I knew what my next book project was. I told her that I had a feeling it would be on menopause, but that I didn't yet have a clear idea on how I would be approaching the subject.

When I told her this, she reflected for a few moments. She then began to describe a vision she was being shown. She said she saw a group of women sitting in a tipi. The women looked distinctly different from one another in both physical appearance and dress. Annette told me that in her vision, one of the women in the tipi communicated with her, saying "they" were "not all there yet" and "it wasn't time yet."

What exactly all this meant was unclear to both of us, but I did somehow get the sense that whatever "it" was, it would not be ready until Spring. Annette confirmed that this is what she sensed also.

A month or two after Annette's first vision, she and I again visited the group of women in the tipi. This time, there were more women, including a very old native woman who looked very much like a spirit grandmother I had encountered when doing soul retrieval work the previous summer.

Soon after, a remarkable series of events began to unfold that would lead me to the knowledge I had been seeking about menopause, wisdom, and power. These events, which occurred during the time I set aside each day for meditation, were profoundly mysterious and enlightening.

This is how it began: One day in December of 1993 during one of my meditations, I decided to return to a place where I had met with spirit guides over the last few years. This return visit proved to be my first step on a journey into the wisdom I sought. The following is an account of that meditation.

*   *   *   *   *

When I arrived at the place where the guides should have been, the landscape had changed. I followed a path up a hill, but when I reached the top, it seemed as though there was nowhere to go from there. I leapt into the air, became an eagle, and flew up into the clouds.

Once in the upper world, I became myself again and started to explore. I came upon a landscape that looked a little like a place I had visited the summer before while on an upper world shamanic journey. On my last journey to this place, there was a tipi in a valley by a stream. I searched for the tipi and found it as before.

As I approached, I saw on the tipi a symbol with which I was somewhat familiar. It was a reverse swastika. I associate this symbol with the wind.

I asked to enter the tipi, and a woman opened the door. She seemed familiar to me, and when I stepped in, I saw that she was the woman who had communicated with my friend Annette Margaret during her vision.

"My name is 'Mariah,'" she said.

She asked me to sit in the East by the door, while she sat opposite me in the West. There were also eight other women in the

6

circle, four in the North and four in the South, although I couldn't see them very clearly. The woman named Mariah indicated that they were all there now but that I was not quite ready.

There was a butterfly painted on the inside of the tipi, and Mariah said, "The butterfly symbolizes change and air, both elements of the wind. All of us have worked with the wind over many eons and dimensions. Wind is movement and change. Menopause, as you call it, is also referred to as 'the change.' Our word for it means 'becoming wise.'"

She painted the reverse swastika on my forehead as some kind of initiation and said, "Return on the first of March and we will be ready to begin."

* * * * *

On March 1, as Mariah had instructed, I entered meditation and, as an eagle, flew up to the upper world, became myself again, and found my way to the tipi.

Mariah asked me to come sit to the right of her in the West as a place of initiation.

She said, "You need to practice being *here* rather than just *seeing yourself here."*

I tried to shift my focus, somewhat successfully, and she then introduced me to the other women in the tipi.

The women seated in the North were from the Northern Hemisphere, and those in the South from the Southern Hemisphere. The information I learned about these women and their origins came mostly from images shown to me rather than spoken words.

On Mariah's left was a woman who looked Nordic, with very blue eyes and gray hair. She will help me with my own heritage. Next to her was a woman from China. I'm not sure about the next one. This woman said something about mixed heritage, but I felt as though she might be from a place close to where I live in Western New York. The last woman in the North was a very old

7

*grandmother from Bear Butte whom I recognized as one who had
given me a crystal tooth during a soul retrieval a friend had done
for me a year earlier.*

*On Mariah's right in the South and sitting next to me was a
woman from Australia—aboriginal. The next one was from South
America—Machu Picchu. Then followed a woman from
Africa—the southern part, like Kenya. The last was East Indian,
from some island south of India. When Mariah spoke of herself,
she said she was from near Hawaii and dated back to the
Lemurian culture.*

*Mariah said, "You will get to know each of us much better. A
lot of the information will come from journeying with these women
so that they can show you things in their own lands. The teachings
will be about the power and wisdom of older women. All of the
women here are Medicine Women of high degree and wish to
teach you the mysteries of their traditions which existed prior to
his-story. Between now and the next time we meet, you should
practice really being present in a journey. We will meet again on
the Spring Equinox, and then the work will begin."*

*   *   *   *   *

By the Spring Equinox, I had developed a method of moving
quickly to the tipi which exists in the upper world. I had a black
and white paint pony with wings, and he carried me there.

*Mariah asked me to sit in the East and to look around and try
to see the other women more clearly. I could do it more easily
with some of the women than with others.*

*Mariah said, "You are moving into a new way of being which
is seeing spirit in all that is around you and moving with it. All of
these women have much to teach you. Their teachings are part of
the records of Earth and must come forward at this time. The
work you did on your previous book with Grandmother Spotted
Eagle shows your readiness for these teachings.*

"You will start with the Nordic woman and then the aboriginal, then the one from China, and so on, spending time journeying with each woman separately from the group and then coming back to the tipi for integration. This process will make many changes in you. Even though you are very busy, it is important to get started now and work on this regularly."

* * * * *

And so it began. Here was the source of information I had been looking for, the course of study I had longed to find. Here were the wisdom teachers from long ago. This book is an account of my journeys with these Grandmothers, Wise Women, and Women of Power.

During this process, which began at the Spring Equinox and ended at the Fall Equinox, I usually worked with the Grandmothers five days a week. Immediately after these meditations, I wrote down, as if in a journal, what I remembered, even when what I had seen or heard was confusing, incomplete, or vague. I wrote down what I saw and heard in just the way I saw and heard it, including the specific words used. I haven't gone back over the text to embellish or change what I originally wrote except for edits which provide clearer meaning for the reader.

I offer the teachings of these Grandmothers and my own learning as a guide for those who wish to embark on their own journey to find the wisdom of "the change."

1

Shadows

When I got on my painted pony today, there was a hooded figure riding double with me. At first I thought I should get rid of it, so I asked it to leave if it was not there for my learning. It did not leave, but I did not see it when I arrived at the tipi.

Mariah introduced me to the Nordic Grandmother who sat on her left. Her name was "Akama." I traveled with Akama to her land which seemed to be a place that had sea to the North and mountains to the South. There were dome-shaped living structures, quite large, each with a smoke hole at the top, in which several families lived around a central fire. The domes were covered with skins and nestled in trees close to a freshwater lake. It was winter there, and Akama said that the families moved closer to the sea in the summer. The lake provided fresh fish in the winter.

Akama said, "There is much to teach you about the women's mysteries and rites. You will take part in some of these here. I am happy that you have come, because this wisdom needs to be passed on to other women. Tomorrow you should come directly here. You will be able to recognize my lodge by the crescent Moon on the front."

The shadow figure was again waiting for me on my horse when I flew to where Akama lived. Again, I asked the figure if it was there for my learning, and I realized that it represented my own shadow side.[1]

I found the symbols on Akama's lodge, and she came out and invited me inside.

We were sitting by the fire on furs drinking tea that tasted like pine when she said, "You need to be more present here."

I shifted my focus from seeing *myself there to* being *there and asked Akama about the shadow figure that was with me.*

She said, "The reason you are here is to participate in an initiation into the Circle of Wise Women, or Medicine Society. In order to prepare for that initiation, you will need to integrate the shadow side. I will help you with the process by showing you ways to work with your shadow.

"We are beginning your journey in the North, in this land, because this is where your ancestors came from long ago. Tracing your father's mother's line back, a very old grandmother of yours lived in this village."

I told her that I had already recently learned some things about my shadow.

She said, "Much of what you have learned so far is about not putting yourself in situations which you really don't want to be in. If you can't go into a situation enthusiastically, you shouldn't be there."

I said that sometimes I feel selfish when I say no.

"There is a distinct difference between taking care of yourself and being selfish. Being able to be present and send energy to people when you are with them is more important than being there all the time.

---

[1] Shadow is usually understood as the rejected or disowned parts of oneself hidden away in the unconscious.

"Let's go for a walk-around to see the community. Each dwelling houses an extended family, and in each family are an elder man and woman who are head of the family. Sometimes they are married and sometimes not. It is not necessarily the oldest person who is chosen. Both age and status are necessary. A person can become old without doing the work to become wise."

We then headed into the woods.

Akama said, "There are sacred places in the woods which are used for learning."

I could see the sacred place of which she spoke before we reached it. It was a pond, and there were also circles of stones and fire circles.

She showed me the pond and said, "If you look at your reflection in the pond, you will see parts of your shadow self which you need to work with."

I looked but couldn't really see much. I was blocking. Finally, I saw myself as a child and got an image of feeling that pleasing people was important.

Akama said, "Continue to pay attention to the reflection throughout the day. Tomorrow you will be meeting with a group of women who will also be initiated."

As I was leaving, I got the sense that the name "Akama" meant "star-filled Sky." I went to my horse and got on, with my shadow, and flew back to the present.

* * * * *

The hooded shadow figure was once again waiting on my horse, and again I asked if it was there for my learning.

This time, the shadow replied and said, "Yes."

I asked it to take off its hood, and when it did, it appeared as Death—the shadow was old habits which need to die. We then headed off to Akama's.

I went into her lodge, and she told me I should change my clothes. She gave me a leather skirt, a fox cape, and winter boots

13

caribou lined with rabbit and fox fur. I felt nice and warm. She said the initiation meeting would be in the women's lodge.

When we went into the lodge, we smudged with something similar to cedar smoke. At first, I saw a circle of women around a large piece of amber, but then the amber became a fire. I joined this inner circle of initiates with, I think, four other women. More women were in an outer circle. I sensed that they passed around an amber nugget as a talking stick to represent the ancient teachings of women.

Akama asked us to begin by talking about what we had learned so far about shadow. Apparently this was the second meeting for the others also. Their first meeting had involved the same teaching that I had yesterday at the pond about identifying parts of the shadow. Akama introduced me as "a woman from another land and time who is here because one of her grandmothers is from this community." The women seemed friendly. They all wore their hair in a fashion similar to the way Akama fixed mine—braided and twisted up on my head.

Each of the initiates in turn began to share what she had seen in her reflection. Each said that the process was frustrating because it is so hard to see the shadow. The shadow represented ways they had learned to behave in childhood, ways which now kept them from being truly themselves. They talked about competition, separateness, and judging others.

When my turn came, I said that there were two things I saw. One was that by being quiet, I could appear intelligent to others and not have the risk of revealing what was really going on for me. The other was that I was always trying to please others and avoid conflict, even to the point of taking responsibility for others.

Akama then asked us to close our eyes, see the pond, and look into it to see our shadows. At first, mine was blurry, but then I saw myself as a little girl with ringlets, at maybe five or six years old. I was playing and climbing trees, riding imaginary horses, fishing for imaginary fish in the stream, and running barefoot through the woods and on the path along the stream. There was no one to share the experience with, no one to tell what it felt like to be sitting in my tree. That part of myself found no voice to express the feeling of joy that came through this connection to nature. I also needed to see others as not knowing in order to see myself as the one who knows in my silence.

Akama said there would be another individual lesson tomorrow and that we would meet together again later. I went out to get on my horse to leave and, instead of the hooded shadow figure, the girl with ringlets was waiting, sitting on the horse. I smiled at her, and it felt good to have her riding behind me as we flew home.

*   *   *   *   *

My child was waiting naked on the winged pony, and I asked her if she wanted some clothes, but she said no. When we arrived, Akama was waiting and gave me furs to put on. She had furs for the child as well. Akama said to bring the child along. We began walking out toward the woods as Akama talked about connection to and respect for all things.

"The children here begin early with an education which the Wise Women insist upon. It honors children's natural ability to connect with all things and gives them a place to talk about it, both in same-sex and mixed groups. That way, girls and boys see that each has something unique to give. These groups are led by a Wise Woman who helps the children learn how to express themselves in an open and honest way and feel good about it.

"You think of your child as a tomboy, yet what she did was the most feminine of things to do—sit in a tree, listen to the wind in the pines, marvel at the flow of the stream, and water the plants

in the garden. She just had no audience for expressing what she was feeling about these things.

"The spider in your dream represents the web of connection which was lost when it became a web of entanglement. Which it becomes depends on intent. As you reclaim this shadow part of yourself, even the bird will sing again as voice is given to the feelings of connection." [2]

When I went back to my horse, the little girl and I got on. I told her that she didn't need to be separate from me, that she could be inside me—then I would be able to more deeply feel her joy and her understanding of connection in all that I do. We flew back home as one.

*   *   *   *   *

As I began to get on my horse, there was something else with me behind my lower back. It seemed like a dark shadow, but for some reason it also felt like a turtle.

I flew to meet Akama, and she said that today we would be using another technique to access shadow. The whatever-behind-my-back came with us. We went to the women's lodge and sat on pillows by the fire. I marveled at the beauty of the lodge.

Akama said, "This lodge carries the energy of many lessons and the women who do ceremony here. Fire is another way to

---

[2] I had recently attended a workshop in which I specifically asked to work on shadow. I immediately received the following dream: I was with a friend who asked me to look through a book to find a picture to show her what I used to look like. I could not find a picture, but she insisted there was one there. I looked through the book again and found a pocket in the back which contained a picture of me with short hair. I pulled the picture out, and onto the table fell a dried-up frog, bird, and spider. I couldn't imagine how I could have left them in there so long. As I looked at them, the frog began to move and come back to life. I took it outside and let it go. Then the bird began to move, but it didn't look good. The spider was in very bad shape.

16

access shadow. By staring into the fire and being receptive, one can see the shadow reflected there. It is time to deal with the dog that was left in the fireplace in your dream.[3]

I stared into the fire and tried to be as receptive as possible. I reviewed the animals that I have known. I couldn't remember anything about a turtle, but the image kept coming back. So I reviewed my relationship with turtles—the small ones we had as pets and let go in the stream, the snapping turtles on the farm, and the ones I stopped to pull out of the road. I thought of myself very young, maybe a year or two old, and wondered if we had a turtle then. When I imagined seeing a turtle from those infant eyes, chills spread all over my body.

I asked whether the turtle had something to do with past life shadow.

"Past life work will come at another time with another Grandmother. We need to focus on clearing the shadow from this lifetime first," Akama said.

I thought about the turtle as well as Samantha, my cat, from the perspective of this life. Akama was encouraging me to look at the point at which my relationship with animals changed. Initially, this relationship seemed to be one of observing animals with delight. Then it changed to wanting animals to do what I wanted them to do. I would touch the turtle's nose to see it withdraw its head. Sam, the cat, represented an uncontrollable animal from the beginning.[4] *She was inconvenient, meowing loudly no matter what I did, insistent on being in the house. It became clear that this change in relationship with animals*

---

[3] I had a dream in which I discovered a dog which had been left in the back of a wood-burning stove. I couldn't imagine how the dog could have been left there, and I didn't think it was mine. But it was still alive and I needed to take it out.

[4] Samantha was a kitten which someone had dropped in front of our house. We found her up a tree with a front leg which didn't work right. Her ear was bent, she had diarrhea, and she was generally quite pathetic.

occurred when I developed the dominating, needing-to-be-in-control part of my personality—a male aspect. I thought of the feminine part we discovered last time, the part which sat in trees and listened to the wind and water but had no voice, and then I thought of the controlling part which wanted everything to obey her. The latter had a voice. This shadow turtle is another reminder of the need to respect all life as it is and to nurture it without trying to change it. It is interesting that it was a turtle I carved when I was learning to work with soapstone recently.

Akama said that next time we would be back in ceremony. As I got on my horse to leave, I could still feel the turtle at my lower back.

* * * * *

I pulled a muscle in my lower back this morning, so I did some healing work on it to help it feel better before journeying.

When I reached my horse, there were no shadow figures there. As I rode, I thought of the turtle of last time at my lower back and also of the child safe inside me. When I got to Akama's, she told me to get on my dress and furs because we were going back to the women's lodge. When I turned back toward my horse, there was a faint shadow figure sitting on the horse where I had been sitting. It was tall and it looked somewhat male, but I wasn't sure. It was like a ghostly figure. Akama said to take it by the hand and bring it along. I was a little concerned about taking this figure into the women's lodge if it was a man. Akama said she didn't think it was a man, and even if it was, it was a part of me, so it was alright. So I took its hand and it followed obediently into the lodge.

I went into the inner circle and sat with the other four women. Behind each of us stood a shadowy figure. In the center was the large amber piece on which the Sun was shining through the smoke hole, casting a golden glow in the lodge. There was a point where I was viewing myself from behind and saw myself as a cat. As I looked around the circle, each woman was an animal, and

18

the shadow behind appeared human. Chills ran through my body as I struggled to understand what was happening. I took a deep breath, focused on a deeper receptivity, and again became me sitting in the circle.

A drum began to beat. It was a drum with a very large diameter, made perhaps from caribou or seal skin. It had a very deep, resonating sound. Akama began to speak.

"The amber light shines on your true essence and casts a shadow. If you move to the drum beat, your shadow will lag behind, and you will catch a glimpse of it. Then turn around and sit facing your shadow."

I did this and invited the shadow to sit with me. The shadow appeared as a skeleton, a Death figure. Akama continued to speak.

"If your shadow appears to you as Death, it is a part which you must let go. It must die. If the shadow appears as an aspect of you, it is to be integrated."

As I looked at the shadow, I saw that it was very docile and obedient. It seemed to represent my views of consensus reality. The reason it was so obedient here is that we were not in consensus reality, and it was afraid to make a move. It appeared almost catatonic. I thought of how this part of me may have developed, concluding that it was probably an enculturation process that did not honor other dimensions. I wondered that my view of consensus reality must die, but this seemed right. This told me that it was holding me back. My consensus reality of the healing of my back was that it would take time. In non-ordinary reality, it can be healed instantly. My consensus view limits my capabilities and possibilities.

Akama told us to take our shadows and turn around so that they were on our laps in front of us facing the amber. As the amber light touched the shadow figures, they began to fade and melt, sighing in a way that indicated a release. When this happened, I felt the energy moving through my body. I put my hands so that the energy would flow to my back, and it seemed as though the other women put their hands near my back also. The drum sounded and we danced while the other women chanted.

When I left to go to my horse, I felt empowered and full of energy.

* * * * *

It was difficult to get focused today. We had just brought home a new puppy, Pooh Bear, who was howling in his cage. Finally he quieted a little.

Akama said we would just go for a walk today, and it would be good practice to focus with all the noise. She said she wanted to talk more about shadow. We went to a clearing in the woods where there was a circle of stones.

"Circles such as this one have been constructed all over the world, and they hold the people's memory of important teachings. Let's look at how our work with shadow is related to the wheel. If the goal of our development or evolution is to be in the center of the wheel, shadow is where we are still attached to the outside. For example, the shadows you have worked with so far are related to the cardinal directions. As you either integrate or let go of the shadow, you move to the center. The closer to the center you are, the more subtle the shadows get. Can you think of what directions the shadows you have worked with so far would be attached to? I know that you are already familiar with the qualities of the directions." [5]

As I thought, I couldn't see it at first, and then it became clear that the child, trusting her feelings, was in the South, while the turtle was in the West, because it represented how I was confusing control and nurturing in my relationship with animals. The shadow

---

[5] I generally think of the East as a masculine place of vision, making things real in the physical world, while the West is feminine, going within to find knowledge. The South is a place of innocence and trust, while the North is the wisdom of the ancestors.

20

figure, which meant letting go of consensus reality, was in the North. Although I was taught consensus reality by my elders, the truth of the ancestors is limitlessness. Akama said the shadow of the East was still to be discovered. There seemed to be a relationship between the South and the West. Both of these aspects had to be integrated, while the North had to be let go.

I asked if the East would also need to be let go.

"Most often it works that way, because the West and South are more feminine aspects, and the North and East are more masculine. There are shadow attachments to the directions of the four winds also, and we will be looking at those later."

I told her how grateful I was to know her and receive these teachings.

She said, "I also am grateful to have someone to pass them on to in your time."

I looked at her and said, "All our relations."

She looked back, knowing that these teachings would be shared with others, and said, "All our relations."

I went to my horse, mounted, and flew back to now, the puppy finally quiet.

* * * * *

Lots of noise from Pooh Bear again today.

I told Akama I was having difficulty staying present. She said we could wait until tomorrow, but I told her I wasn't sure it would be any quieter then. So we got started on the East shadow. We went to the top of a hill to watch the Sun rise.

Akama said, "Notice how it begins with a little light followed by pink. Then you begin to see the Sun peek up. It looks so large and magnificent when it first comes up, but once the Sun has risen, it looks smaller until time for setting, when it again becomes large. So it is with visions. They look quite magnificent at the beginning and end, but the in-between is often quite boring, tedious work. It is important to stay in the moment during this time and do the work in a disciplined but joyful way."

I asked what the shadow looks like here. I know that it is called Boredom and Bad Attitude, but I could still not see it. We decided to try again tomorrow. I almost forgot to fly back.

*   *   *   *   *

I had a hard time focusing again even though Pooh Bear was sleeping by my side.

When I told Akama that I was having difficulty, she said focus was part of the East shadow. We went to the women's lodge and sat by the large piece of amber. I looked and could not see anything, but the sunlight on the amber made it glow and radiate a beautiful golden light.

She said, "Your colors are this golden amber and deep purple. The lessons of the East shadow are related to the third eye."

I remembered the teaching of yesterday regarding the Sun, since the amber looked like the rising Sun. As I continued to look at the amber, I saw in my reflection some black, gloppy stuff—very sticky. This image portrayed my not wanting to move forward with something—procrastination.

Akama said, "Gather this up in your body and hold it out for the amber light to shine on. The sticky stuff keeps you from being fully focused on a task and carrying it through."

As I held the sticky stuff out, the light dissolved it. Then I looked again and saw within me a ball, bouncing all over. It represented the way I jump from one thing to another and then another. This keeps me from focusing on and completing things. As I caught the ball in my right hand, the power to jump to other things was transferred to my hand. I held the ball to the light and it faded. My hand now would control when it is time to do something else.

I asked if there were more images, and she said, "Probably, but remember that each will become a little more subtle."

22

I looked again and saw my fear of new things and my fear of things not coming out as I want. My fear appeared white within my body—a white figure looking scared. I brought the figure out and held it to the amber light to be dissolved.

I asked again if there was more, and Akama said, "One more."

I looked again, and with Akama's help, saw how I get tired or sick to keep from focusing on a task. I got an image of an old man who was tired, but I also thought of my mother's "poor me" role. I called the tired sick man forward to be released into the light.

Akama suggested getting some amber to wear to remind me of this teaching as I focus on a task.

I thanked her and she said, "We will be in ceremony next time. Our work will continue for another week as we work with the shadows of the four winds."

*　　*　　*　　*　　*

It's the first day of my moontime today, and I am feeling a little scattered with my focus.

When I arrived at Akama's, I went into the lodge and dressed in leggings and boots trimmed with fur and some kind of sparkly beads. I wore a soft, hide dress and a fur jacket. Akama acknowledged that it was my moontime and gave me a pad of mosses covered in soft buckskin which was very comfortable. My hair was braided and wrapped into a bun.

On my way to the lodge, I kept losing focus. Finally, when I was able to stay present, Akama told me and four other women that we were going to learn a song and dance to integrate our learning about the shadows of the four directions. We were in a circle around the large piece of amber. The amber was casting a golden light reflected from the Sun shining through the smoke hole. The golden light was leaving our shadows on the back wall of the lodge. We were to face our shadow in a particular direction, hold our hands above our head, clap twice, and in the

23

South and West, turn clockwise to pull the shadow in, and in the North and East, turn counterclockwise to let it go.

While we were doing this, we sang the song and thought of our shadows of the four directions. At first the song was words I did not understand, but gradually, as I danced, I became aware of the meaning of the song:

> Shadow (clap, clap), lead me to my wisdom,
> Shadow (clap, clap), you're everywhere I go.
> Shadow (clap, clap), come live within my wisdom,
> Shadow (clap, clap), become the golden light."

I danced and sang while picturing my shadows of the four directions and the teachings they have offered me.

*   *   *   *   *

Akama met me outside the lodge today. She said that we would go for a walk and talk about the four winds. We went along the lake and walked to an open field at the end of the lake. She began to talk about the winds.

"In some views, the four winds are the same as the four cardinal directions, while in others, they are slightly rotated to become Northeast, Southeast, Northwest, and Southwest. That is the system you are familiar with, is it not? In this latter system, the winds move like a figure eight. Each wind has both a direction it is blowing from and a direction it is blowing to. The system I am teaching you is a little different from the one you are familiar with. In this one, the winds can move in a figure eight in either direction around the wheel.

"Let's talk about the qualities of each of the four winds. In the Northwest is decay, while the Southeast is full growth. As you can see, they are quite opposite processes. Movement can occur from decay to full growth or from full growth to decay. In the Northeast are beginnings, and the Southwest is completion. Again, we can move from beginnings to completion or from completion to

24

beginnings. *A figure eight might go from decay to beginnings to completion to full growth to decay."*

I'm not sure this makes sense to me. Shouldn't things go from beginnings to growth to completion to decay?

"That is what linear thinking would tell us, but process is not linear, it is circular, looping backwards and forwards. There are many times that decay of something leads directly to new growth, and many times where beginnings require a vision of completion before growth can occur. And, of course, growth can lead us to find that which must be let go of—decay—in order for new beginnings to happen. As I said before, the movement can also occur in the opposite direction. Decay leads to growth, growth to completion, completion to new beginnings, and beginnings to decay and back to growth."

I think I'm beginning to understand this. And you are right, it is never a linear progression.

"There is another movement of the winds where we would see the eight on its side. For example, here decay could lead to growth, leading to beginnings, leading to completion, leading to decay, and back to growth. Or the reverse movement: completion to beginnings, to growth, to decay, to completion. Seeing the movement in this way helps to see the wind directions as complementary rather than opposite. Both the 'to' and 'from' directions are necessary for movement. Tomorrow we will begin looking for the shadows of the four winds."

You mean we will find a shadow for each of these qualities?

"There is a shadow that blocks beginnings, one that blocks completions, one that blocks growth, and one that blocks decay. We will come back to this field, and using it as center, you will move off to each of the wind directions to listen to what the wind in that direction has to say of your shadow."

This sounds exciting. I have been very aware of the music of the wind lately as it plays symphonies through the grasses and trees.

Akama said, "The wind is a great musician and you should always be aware of its song, since it is your name."

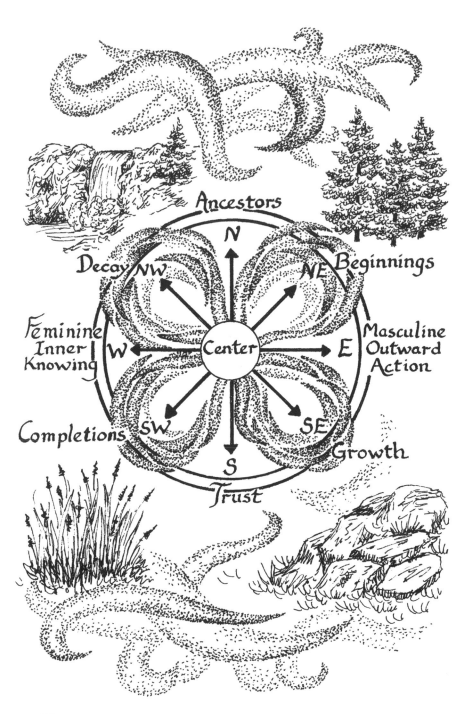

We walked back along the lake, and I found myself being pulled upward, seeing everything from above. I called my horse as I continued rising, seeing the Earth from above, and then I flew home.

*   *   *   *   *

I started feeling very nauseous after my yoga and spinning. I took a shower and ate a banana, but I felt worse. When I started to meditate, I felt a little better but very sleepy. I did a little healing work and then went to see Akama.

We walked along the lake to the meadow. I was having a very hard time staying focused. Before we began, I asked her about how I was feeling. She said something about cleansing and my body adjusting to a new vibrational rate. I tried to focus on the winds, but I felt as though I was on the edge of sleep and dreaming.

From the center of the meadow, I went to the Northeast to the place where the pine trees stood. I went into the pines and sat, leaning up against a tree in a circle of pines, and tried to listen to what the wind was saying. It was about beginnings, having a good attitude, staying focused, listening, not limiting things. But I couldn't really see how shadow fit in, other than it being what blocks these things. The sound of the wind in the pines was made by the air moving over each needle—and there are so many needles, perhaps like so many possibilities. I am still not sure what the shadow is, and I've been gone a very long time.

I went back to the meadow where Akama was. She said all was fine and would become clearer tomorrow. I went back to my horse and flew back.

I lay down and slept.

*   *   *   *   *

I am feeling much better and more alert today.

I went to my horse and jumped on, but he wouldn't move. I tried again, but he still wouldn't move. I asked him why we weren't moving, and he said it was because I was thinking of him as a real horse. It was true. I was seeing him in great detail as a physical horse.

But you are real in this dimension, I said.

So we chatted a bit and he wanted me to really look at him. He is black and white with wings. He said his name is Cloud Dancer. Finally, we headed off through the Sky. We agreed that if I were anywhere and wanted him, I would whistle and he would come.

I met Akama outside her lodge, and we walked along the lake to the field. I told her I felt much better today and thanked her for her help yesterday. She said that I had entered a healing dimension and that had helped my body to heal. As we walked along the lake, I got a sense of needing to draw a map of the area. We went into the field to the large rock which marked the center of our circle. Akama said I should go off to the Northeast again to listen to the wind in the pines.

I went to the same place I was yesterday and sat down in the circle of pines, leaning against a large tree. I thanked the trees for nurturing me yesterday and said that I was more able to listen to the wind about beginnings today and that I remembered what was said yesterday. The wind began to tell me about beginnings.

"There are two things which interfere with beginnings. One is your fear that what you begin won't be something you will really be able to do or that it won't come out the way you want it to. This leads to needing to know a lot of information about something before you do it. The other is limiting, or feeling that you need to limit the possibilities. There are times when you walk around trying to decide what to begin, consumed in mental decision making. Both of these problems are surmounted by listening. Let the next beginning call you and don't think about its outcome. Just

28

listen for its calling. That way, you are open to all the possible beginnings, not just the ones you can think of. It also allows you to stay open to many outcomes from the same beginning."

So, let me see if I understand correctly. The shadow is fear and limited thinking. I can see how I learned those as a child, limiting what I attempted in order to make sure I was successful. But also many times I couldn't decide—and still can't—what to begin. The way to integrate this shadow is to listen for the beginning—whatever it might be—to call me without judging its possible outcomes.

"Yes, you have understood this teaching."

Thank you, Wind Through the Pines, for teaching me about listening for beginnings.

I headed back to where Akama was waiting at the rock in the center of the field. She said that I should now go to the Southwest to listen to what the winds have to say about completion.

I walked down through the field toward the lake, looking for the right spot. I finally sat in the field of grasses and watched the wind blow the grasses so that they looked like waves. Then the wind began to speak.

"The shadow of completions is ego. Completion should never be thought of as a final step but only as a crest of a wave. Sometimes it is too easy to see this completed work as something you have done, yet in reality, you as a separate entity do nothing."

Are you speaking of the importance of being humble?

"It is more than humble. As you watch the beautiful dance of the grasses in the wind, what is it that the grass is doing? It is only being flexible and allowing the wind to blow through it. The dance, the movement, is created by the surrender of the grass to the will of the wind. Without either piece, the dance would not occur. So it is with your completions. This point in the motion could not occur without your flexible surrender to the process, to spirit moving through you. When ego takes credit for the process, it is like grass that becomes inflexible and brittle, standing straight

up by itself, saying 'look at me,' rather than moving with the flow. It will soon be broken in the wind."

So, if the shadow of completions is ego, what is the word for the integration?

"I am not sure what word you would use to describe this, since many words—'surrender,' 'flow,' 'flexible'—capture a little of what this means. Probably 'oneness' would be good as a reminder that movement of spirit through you is what brings completion."

Thank you, Wind in the Grass, for this teaching. I went back to meet Akama and together we walked back along the lake. I whistled for Cloud Dancer and mounted. Akama said that we would work with the other directions tomorrow.

* * * * *

I called for Cloud Dancer and we were off to Akama's. He wanted to follow as we walked along the lake. Akama remarked about what a beautiful animal he was. I told him to wait until I whistled. We walked back to the rock in the field.

Akama said that from yesterday's beginnings and completions, we would move to growth in the Southeast. So I walked off in that direction. The ground rose steeply to rocky ledges. I climbed up to the ledge which overlooked the field facing Northwest. The wind whistled through the rocks from behind me. The puppy had not yet fallen asleep and came over to jump on me. I lost my concentration for a moment until he wandered off. It became clear that the shadow for growth was distraction, and that the opposite, integration, was focus. I continued to be distracted by the puppy a few more times and then began to ask the wind to tell me more about this lesson.

"Focus requires intention, and intention requires clarity and passion. Without these, growth stops when distractions come up. If a flower were distracted from taking in the sunlight, rain, and nutrients, it would stop growing. Humans also cease to grow when distracted from purpose. When this happens, sometimes you need to move counterclockwise to beginnings to listen and get clear

30

again. Or, you might move clockwise to completion to get a vision of oneness and flow. You could also move across the circle to decay to let go of the distraction. Any of the four winds can be accessed from any point on the circle. Distractions come in many forms—there are physical distractions, emotional distractions, mental distractions, and spiritual distractions. Be clear with passion, and distractions will not be a block to growth."

Is there anything that will help me specifically with the process of focusing?

"Remember that it is a process. Your focus is much better now than it was before. It will continue to improve as you clear away shadows and become more aware."

Thank you, Wind Through the Rocks. I am grateful for this lesson.

At some point during this experience, I decided to focus my intention on sending some energy to the puppy to heal his throat of the cough he had. I could feel his little body sucking in the energy.

I went back down into the field where Akama waited. She said I would go to the Northwest next time, and then we would be in ceremony after that.

She said, "Remember that whenever you move across the circle, you move through the center—self and Universe. We will talk more about that later."

I thanked her and whistled for Cloud Dancer as we began to walk back. Then, I was on his back and drifting out somewhere, but I felt a strong pull back to now.

Later in the day, I went to find some amber as Akama had instructed me to do. The only amber in the store was a small ball with silver around it. The silver was shaped into stars and crescent Moons. I thought that was interesting, since the sign on Akama's lodge is the crescent Moon and her name means "starry night." The amber is now on a chain around my neck.

*   *   *   *   *

It is thundering today.

I flew on Cloud Dancer over the Thunder Beings to meet Akama. I felt good and excited being there to learn about the shadow of decay.

When we got to the field, Akama pointed to the Northwest and said, "There is a creek that runs down to the lake and a spot where there is a waterfall. The wind blows there with an interesting sound. You will know the place when you get there."

I told her I had already been anticipating this direction and thought there would be a waterfall.

She said, "Good. You are using your intuition."

I started across the field and came to the creek. The place I had pictured had trees around it and was in a ravine, but what I saw was a rather tall waterfall over the side of a hill with no trees. At the bottom was a rock which looked like a good place to sit. I hesitated a little, wondering if I didn't need to follow the stream higher to find the place with trees, and then decided that if this was what I came upon first, then it must be the place. I climbed down and sat on the rock and was surprised that I was sitting in the Sun. I thought the place of decay would be darker. As I listened for the wind, it did seem to make a noise as it blew across the side of the hill. Then, as I was looking at the water, I noticed that there was a cave behind the waterfall. I stepped inside, getting only a little wet in the process. The cave was dark and seemed to go deep into the earth. The wind blew out of the cave, making a loud, wailing sound. Between that and looking out through the water tumbling down from the falls, I felt very sad.

I asked the wind from the cave to teach me the lesson of decay.

It said, "The shadow of decay and loss is holding on, of course. Holding on rather than letting go and releasing. Decay is an opposite process to growth and just as important. Rather than holding on, you should embrace and release what you are losing, for in the larger picture there is no loss. What you are releasing is now free to go on to teach others and become part of their journey or, in its transformation, to provide energy for the Universe. Holding on when you need to be letting go not only disrupts the flow within you, it also disrupts the flow of the Universe. The decay process is also a destruction or de-construction process. There are many times as you move through the growth process that things must be rearranged. Sometimes it is just a restructuring of what has already grown, and other times something must be removed. There are still other places in the process where large pieces must be released.

"Whatever form the decay takes, this process is most appropriate at the time of bleeding or the new Moon. Since this is a time of physical release within your body, it is a natural time to release on other levels. If this were done on a monthly basis, then not so much would build up to be released all at once. As you become a Wise Woman and hold your blood and power, you have full access to the power of decay at any time, both to see it clearly in others as well as in yourself."

If decay is a good process, why does it sound as though you are wailing and feel as though you are crying?

"The moaning sound I make could also be thought of as toning. The vibration which is created when we are making a sound can aid in the process of letting go. In releasing a particular thing, one should find its sound, its vibration, and then make that sound part of the releasing process. If you don't know the vibration of what you are releasing, make sounds until you find the right one.

"There is often emotion attached to what is being released, and the tears wash away its vibration once it is released. Humans would not have been given the capacity to cry if crying was not important for them to do. It is part of a cleansing process associated with decay. There is a joy of releasing as you give away to others and to the Universe, and releasing should always be done with love. Since you are a part of everything, and everything in the Universe is a part of you, nothing is truly lost."

Thank you, Wind in the Cave, for this teaching. I will come to you when I am in decay process to hear your beautiful voice reminding me to release with love.

I ducked under the waterfall and headed up the hill to where Akama was waiting.

Seeing that I was a little wet, she said, "I see that you found the right place."

I said I had and that it was not where I thought it was.

She smiled and said, "Come, sit on this rock which marks the center of the circle of the four winds. This center is your center, your true essence. When you move with the wind directly across the center, it is a quick and powerful movement, because it always goes through your essence. While the movement of the winds loops around in figure eights for many things and through most of our lives, as a Wisdom Woman you will spend more time remaining in the center, because it is from this position that you have access to all the winds at once. You can move in any direction very quickly from center and can have the clarity to see which process needs to be engaged. It is more like being the director of the process rather than allowing the process to direct you. I might remind you that this director role is not played by your mind but by your essence at your center. As you become more conscious and aware, you will be more able to consciously stand in your essence. Next time, we will be in ceremony, so be sure to wear your amber, and it would also be good to wear your otter necklace."

Oh, I hadn't thought of that, but it would be good. I whistled for Cloud Dancer and began my way back. I felt very deep and seemed to hover just above my body before being fully in it.

*   *   *   *   *

I called to Cloud Dancer and flew off to meet Akama. When I got there, she took the five of us to the reflecting pond in the woods. We all undressed and bathed in the pond. The water was warm like a hot spring. We were given herbs to rub on our bodies as a cleansing. When I came out, Akama twisted and braided my hair, and I dressed in my hide dress and boots trimmed with white Arctic fox fur. She placed a black shawl around my shoulders and the fur of a white otter around my neck.

She said, "This white otter lived here for many years and was a grandmother to my tribe—a teacher not only for the otter tribe, but a spirit guide for the humans as well. The black and white together are the West and North on the wheel and represent that period in your life,[6] but they are also opposite colors and represent the wisdom of holding or bridging the opposites. The Wise Woman stands in the center and thus holds the opposites."

I went with the other women and Akama to the women's lodge. We were in the center circle, again around the amber piece. In a larger circle around us were the Wise Women. Around them were the women who were still bleeding and of childbearing years, and in a circle outside them were the girls who had not yet had their first moontime. Akama was leading the ceremony.

She said all five of us were from other dimensions and were here to learn about the wisdom time. As I looked at the other women, most had graying blonde or brown hair with blue or green eyes. One had brown eyes. Akama called me up in front of her and spoke to me.

"You are Otter Woman. Otter is a powerful teacher about the joy of being and, as a water animal, that the joy is in the feeling of being. Your otter spirit has curled up on your crown chakra and is ready to lead you to other realms. The white otter brings the energy which will guide your Wise Woman years, showing others the joy of being in feeling. So you are known to us as Otter Woman."

I sat down and the next woman got up. She had an Arctic fox fur around her neck.

Akama said, "You are Fox Woman. The fox teaches the wisdom of being clever. As you return to your people, your cleverness will be needed by women to bring the feminine more fully into your culture."

---

[6] In my understanding of the Wheel of Life, West represents the time of older adulthood, while North is the place of death and rebirth, the ancestors, and wisdom.

The next woman had reindeer fur around her neck.

"You shall be called Reindeer Woman. Reindeer gives away to nourish the people, clothe them, and provide hide for their shelters and drums. You carry the medicine of nurturing to your people so they may learn to nurture each other."

Another woman had white rabbit fur on her neck.

"As Rabbit Woman, you carry many lessons to the people at this time. Rabbit gives away to many predators for their food. To give away the flesh without fear is a powerful lesson. It can be done only when one knows one's place in the larger scheme of the Universe. Many will give up their physical bodies in this time, and rabbit teaches the need for trust in the process rather than fear. You will help many to cross over."

The last woman had a ring of feathers around her neck.

"Eagle Woman has the wisdom of flying high and bringing the truths of the Universe to the people. You will fly high into the other dimensions to retrieve knowledge for your people."

I looked at Akama, wanting to see who she was, and I saw her as the snowy owl—Owl Woman.

"All of you have learned the lessons of shadow. Wise Women, Medicine Women, Shaman Women no longer cast shadows. As the Sun itself does not cast a shadow, neither will you, because you have become the source of the light. The amber you each are wearing is a symbol for the golden light that shines from within you to the far corners of your being so that each shadow is transformed from darkness to light. Your shadows are not completely gone at this point, but they are all in the light. The Wise Woman is not only the source of the golden light, but she stands in the center, her essence, which is the center of the Universe, and stays there, holding the energy of the opposites—light and dark, summer and winter, spring and fall, male and female, beginning and completion, growth and decay. As she moves from her center, her essence, she speaks and does those things which are authentically her. She shares the gift of the golden light and her wisdom with her people."

We began to dance, and as we did, we each became the animal of our name. The song was:

Wisdom Woman, I stand within my center,
Wisdom Woman, I am the golden light.

Akama said we would be headed back to other realities tomorrow, but we could always come back or call on her if we needed her. I thanked Akama and said I would see her in the tipi tomorrow.

*   *   *   *   *

Cloud Dancer and I flew off to the tipi. I waited at the door and then entered when told to do so. I sat close to the door and looked around at the women.

Mariah said, "Heron Wind, also known as Otter Woman, is here."

I wore my clothing from yesterday's ceremony and had on the amber and my otter necklace. I saw Akama and we smiled at each other. Mariah began to speak.

"I see that you have learned many things from your journey with Akama. I can see the golden light within you."

Yes, I said, I am very grateful for the teachings.

I thought I should have something to give Akama in return. I told her that I would promise to share the teachings with other women. I knew that would please her.

I asked Mariah about the form of the book.

She said, "You are correct in assuming that you will begin the writing process about each journey as you complete the journey with that woman. Today completes your work with Akama, so you may begin the writing process tomorrow. We will be helping you with the writing, so do not worry about the form."

I said I already concluded that I could not figure it out with my mind because my mind did not have access to all the information.

Mariah asked me to move into the center of the tipi and dance while they played music and chanted. As I did so, all the women brought out instruments from their own cultures. Akama had her large drum, and there were many other instruments I did not recognize. The music was complex and beautiful. I danced the things I had learned. I danced the golden light and, from within me, illuminated the tipi. I danced the four directions and the four winds. I felt like the grasses of the Southwest, surrendering to the spirit dancing through me. As I danced to the Northwest, the tears began to flow.

At some point in the dancing, I realized that the rhythm followed my movements rather than my movements following the rhythm. I experimented a little by dancing slower, then faster, and then I stopped. The music and rhythm followed my actions.

At first I thought: How can this be? If I am surrendering to spirit dancing through me, how can my action control the rhythm? But then I understood that I was being taught about how my action controls the vibration around me. Spirit moves through me into action, and action creates vibrations. As I learn to move with greater consciousness and intention, the music and rhythms I create around me will be more beautiful.

After I achieved that understanding, Mariah asked me to lie down on furs which were in front of her. While the rhythms continued softly, each woman, beginning with the very old woman in the Northeast, came over to me and ran her hands over my body. The first one went from my head to my feet and occasionally seemed to be picking something out. The next three also went from head to feet. Mariah put one hand on each side of my body and seemed to be balancing left and right, up and down. The next four, who sit in the South, went from my feet to my head. I could feel the energy from all of them. When Akama went over me with her hands, I could feel the golden light become brilliant.

Mariah said that this would help to integrate the teachings more fully into my body.

She said that tomorrow I would meet the woman from Australia on her right. I still felt I should give Akama a gift. I went to her and gave her a small Herkimer diamond, because it is from a place near where I live, and I told her that it represents the seed of wisdom she has placed within me. I thanked the Grandmothers and they acknowledged me as sister.

I went out and mounted Cloud Dancer to fly back to now.

2

Dreamtime

When I flew off on Cloud Dancer, my dog Tigger was sleeping next to me and went along. We entered the tipi, and Tigger stayed sitting in my place by the door while I went over to Mariah.

Mariah introduced me to the Australian woman and said, "You need to remember that all of these women are from cultures that existed long ago, before the written records were kept, although there are records in many other forms. So, the aboriginal culture and teachings do not remain today except in the memory of a very few. This is why it is important to bring this wisdom back to the people of Earth."

This woman was very dark-skinned and a little shorter than I am. I listened very carefully as she said her name, "Calama," with the emphasis on the "ma," and the a's pronounced as "ah." She said I should go with her now so I would know where to meet her tomorrow.

Mariah said, "Don't forget to come back to the tipi to get your dog and horse."

I took Calama's hand and we flew through the Sky very high, with Earth appearing as a small globe below us. We came down in Australia on a very large, red plateau which could be seen from a long way away. I thought that this place must be Ayer's Rock.

I had heard about Ayer's Rock four years ago when a friend had given me a pouch she made which had sand in it from there.

Calama confirmed that this was the name given to this place long after her time.

She said, "This is a place used for many hundreds of years by my people for ceremony. I want to show you this circle worn in the ground here, like a Medicine Wheel worn into the stone from the many feet who danced here. Red is the color of the blood of Earth, the blood of women, the creative force from which all is born. This is a special, sacred place for women but also for all the people to come to listen to the knowledge of the Universe. We hear the history from the rocks themselves which hold the memory for events of long ago when the Earth was born. The rocks hold the history of humans as well. We also hear the future as we gaze out into the Universe around us. Sky Beings come here to teach us of the mysteries. The wisdom of the Dreamtime is sacred knowledge to my people, and this is what you have come here to learn. Dreamtime is the place where all can be seen as it really is, beyond the illusion of the everyday perception.

"Sometimes you and I will journey alone and other times we will join with other women. You will have an opportunity to listen for the past and the future here on this red rock also. I want you to remember your dreams while we are working together so that you can relate them to me when we meet. So, we will meet here in this circle tomorrow."

She said she would go with me back to the tipi, so we flew hand in hand over the Earth. I smiled at Calama, Mariah, and Akama, thanking them. I nodded to the other women and went back to get Tigger who was patiently sitting and wagging her tail. We went outside the tipi. I got on Cloud Dancer, Tigger jumped up behind, and we flew back to now.

*   *   *   *   *

That night I was very busy in my dreams. Early in the night I had a dream I can't remember very well, but I think I was being taught something because it was one of those dreams where I wake up with a wow! feeling and an image of expansion which I can't quite remember.

In the second dream, I was with a group, maybe five or six people, and I was teaching about shadow. I was making a list of their names and phone numbers, and I put quite a few blanks at the bottom because there would be new people joining us. Then there seemed to be more people and the majority of them were men. As I taught them, I used many examples from my own growth process and I wondered whether it was getting to be too much, but they seemed okay with it. It seemed as though the people I was teaching were just beginning to learn about how to do this work, sort of like the students I teach in college or like some of my clients. It seemed as though we were moving toward a point where I was going to teach them something profound, and I was judging whether they were ready. In some ways, it felt like the same thing that I was taught in the first dream.

The last dream took place on a farm somewhat like the one I used to live on, in that there was a large, old-fashioned barn with a loft. I went into some kind of bathroom in the barn to wash my hands and did not realize that there was a man in the bathtub. He cleared his throat and I was surprised to see him there. I didn't know who he was and considered whether I should be afraid of him and decided not. I went back out and saw him again later. I found out that he was living in the loft of my barn and was a homeless person by choice—he had no job. There was a woman living in the other side of the loft as well. I got to know these two by talking to them and they seemed like nice people. They were moving North for the summer or something like that, but would be back. There was also something about a young man who was working in the fields too, but I can't remember what.

When I flew off to where I was to meet Calama, the large, red rock plateau could be seen from a long way away. I landed and Calama was standing next to the circle worn in the stone. She said to come into the circle and told me that today we would talk about what the Dreamtime is.

"Dreamtime is like the void from which all things come into physical being. All things in the Universe exist there. It is like the doorway to the Universe through which one can access all knowledge. When you first begin to dream at night, your soul returns home to be in the Dreamtime again and to feel all the love and to know everything. The feeling you had upon waking—of being taught or an image of expansion—is the leftover memory, still drifting in your consciousness, of being in the Dreamtime.

"In many ways, the Dreamtime includes all that you call non-ordinary reality, but when you access it through journey work, you do not perceive it in its entirety. One of the things we need to work on is improving your conscious memory and experience of the Dreamtime.

"As you move through the night, you have dreams which can give you a glimpse of the future as well as ones which are symbolic of your process. These are more individual or personal dreams, where the Dreamtime itself is universal. You did fairly well last night gathering dreams which represent these different experiences. The first was a vague awareness of the Dreamtime. The second was a dream of the future, teaching those things which you want most to teach. You will start with a few but more will be coming. Your feeling about teaching using your own experience is important for, in truth, that is all anyone can teach. And you will be teaching many men, as they need to learn about the mysteries even more than women. Your last dream was more symbolic about parts of yourself. You were unaware of shadow parts that you had rejected but now find them interesting and nice enough. I will let you contemplate what part of your shadow they represent.

"I want you to sit in this circle now and let your intentions be known that you wish to be more consciously aware of the Dreamtime and remember your soul visits there."

As I sat, I felt connected to all who had come to this spot before me to learn. Calama then led me down a path which ran beside a stone wall. On the wall were many symbols carved in the stone.

"These are symbols brought back from the Dreamtime by seekers such as yourself. They are all different and pieces of the possible. You will have an opportunity to carve your own symbol and will learn to understand those placed here by others."

I looked out over the desert and saw some rocks rising into a butte. It was so beautiful there!

Calama led me back up the trail and said, "Meet me back here next time and we will do some traveling. In the meantime, try to stay aware that the Dreamtime exists simultaneously with the physical reality and always holds all possibilities."

* * * * *

I had a difficult time focusing today—so many things to do.

I met Calama on the red rock at the circle. I was barefoot and wearing a reddish brown cloth tied up over one shoulder. Calama was dressed in the same way.

She said, "You have had some dreams which you do not know the meaning of. Just keep writing them down. They will become clearer to you later. You have been anticipating our lessons, and while you get glimpses of them, you can only see that which your conscious mind has access to when you are thinking about it. That is why things are often different than you expect. We are headed down on the flat where the water hole is. See that group of bushes and trees?"

I saw the place she pointed to in the distance. We began walking on a path down off the rocks and then across the sands to the water hole.

"I want you to sit in the spot beneath that tree."

I said that it was a very small tree.

She said, "It is small but old. Because it is dry here, the tree does not grow much each year."

There was some kind of hut there, but she said, "Since you are not staying a long time, we do not need to talk about that. Most of the time huts are not used for sleeping, only a wrap under the stars. Sit there by yourself and stay alert. I will be back in a little while, and you can tell me everything you have seen."

So I sat and watched. At first I stared at the pool of water and thought about what water is. It is the blood of life as air is the breath. We are made mostly of water in our physical form as are many other things around us. As I looked, I saw what appeared to be vapor coming up out of the water and rising into the Sky. I realized that I was seeing the evaporation of the water which might later form Clouds.

Then there were several aborigines who walked up to the water and drank, filled small containers and then moved on. After a time, a white woman came in from the other side,—the right—looked around, and threw two tablets into the water. I thought about what they were and saw everything around the water hole dying, including the animals and people who drank from it. But then an aboriginal woman came in from the same direction, as if she been watching the white woman, and reached down into the water and grabbed the two tablets. She looked at them and took them with her out into the sand and buried them some distance away. She then continued on her journey, following the white woman.

I thought about where the water came from and followed it down into the earth. I was sitting there, trying to figure out what all of this had to do with the Dreamtime, when Calama appeared. I told her what I had seen and she explained.

"You sat in the present moment and were able to see what had happened here in the past, what the future might be, along with the most probable future, and how that could be changed. You also saw beyond what your eyes were able to sense by seeing the evaporation of water and tracing the water to the underground stream. You saw with your third eye—Dreamtime eye—beyond

what your two eyes could tell you. If you only observed with your two eyes, you would have told me that nothing had happened here while I was gone. You can do this in any moment of your physical reality—look beyond the physical with your third eye to see the Dreamtime. I want you to practice this, because the next time we meet you will need this skill. Meet me on the rock by the circle tomorrow, since we will be headed off in a different direction."

I thanked her for the teaching and started to come back. I almost forgot to call Cloud Dancer and fly back.

*   *   *   *   *

I ate too much chocolate cake at a birthday party last night and was very sick today—feeling toxic. I had a dream last night that a phone was disconnected. I didn't journey today because I felt so sick. Felt better the next day and went to meet Calama at the circle on the red rock.

When I started to get off the horse, I kept falling and was having trouble standing up. I told myself to get centered.

I told Calama that I was sorry I was not there yesterday and that I already heard what she had to say about it—that there was something in the last lesson that I found difficult to digest. I also said that I had been working with it and I had many questions. I had the experience of looking out onto the lawn at home and seeing deer when there were no physical deer there. It happened again when I was at the Medicine Wheel. [1]

She said she would like to hear my questions but that most of the answers will come through my own experience.

I said that I wanted to know how to tell what kind of Dreamtime image I am seeing. Is it something which occurred in that space in an earlier time? Or maybe will occur in the future?

---

[1] On the hill above my house, I constructed a circle of stones fashioned after a Sun Bear's Medicine Wheel.

Is it something which exists in another space or dimension or is it a projection from my own mind?

She said, "Those are difficult questions to answer when you have just been introduced to the Dreamtime. The answers come with experience—sort of the wisdom to know the difference. I will say that you have already learned about the intentional projection from your mind and that is how things in the Dreamtime can be changed or brought forward.[2] For now, I want you to follow me as we walk through these hills and try to see into the Dreamtime as we go."

We started off in the opposite direction from where we went last time. As we walked, I saw different things and told Calama what I was seeing. First, I saw a depression in the ground that was filled with water, but I could not tell whether it existed in the past or future. Then I saw a tiger, and Calama commented that there are no tigers in Australia. I guessed that it must be from another space or dimension. It came and walked beside me, and I recognized it as the tiger of my emotional chakra.

Then we came to a place where I saw the entrance to a cave.

Calama said, "Good. This cave entrance exists only in the Dreamtime. If it existed in ordinary reality, it could be misused. Only those who can see the Dreamtime may enter. Of course, that does not mean that sorcerers could not enter, but at least they respect the dimension involved."

She indicated that I should enter the cave. I was having a very difficult time staying present just standing beside it. It was almost like drifting off to sleep with different dream images coming in.

She finally said, "You need to stay conscious during this process," and took my hand as we stepped into the cave.

---

[2] Last summer, I learned exercises which involve projecting an image of myself, while walking, to a point some distance ahead of my physical body and then walking into the image and paying attention to the feeling when my physical body merges with the image.

48

It seemed like a swirling cloud or mist as I looked at the top of the cave. It was like looking at the Milky Way galaxy. I was drifting off again when I felt her take my hand and we stepped back out of the cave.

She said, "That is enough for now. We will work with this again tomorrow. Find your way back to the cave using your Dreamtime vision."

I already knew that there would be a marker that could be seen from a long way away in the Dreamtime.

*   *   *   *   *

When I was quite far away, I could see where the cave was. There was a white ring around it and it also seemed to shine. I found the entrance but did not see Calama.

Then I heard her voice saying, "I'm in here. Come on in."

I stepped through the entrance and sat down on a rock next to Calama to let my eyes adjust. I looked up into what appeared to be the night Sky and a swirling galaxy. Calama motioned for me to follow, and we walked a short distance to where there was a spiral, something like what might be seen inside a seashell. She stepped onto the spiral and I followed. It was a slide and we slid around the spiral down into the Earth. The slide dropped us with a splash into a hot pool of water. It was fairly deep but I could stand up. We swam over to the side and pulled ourselves up onto the side and sat.

Calama told me to look around. When I did, I saw other women also sitting around the pool. All appeared to be older aboriginal women, maybe twelve in all.

Calama said, "This is a sacred pool used by women for cleansing and ceremony. The hot mineral waters are healing."

I asked whether this was a Dreamtime pool or if it exists in the physical world.

She said, "It is a combination. The pool itself is physical, but the spiral slide was created by us from the Dreamtime to put a little more fun in the entrance. We need to get back in the water now."

All the women moved into the water and washed, then climbed out and moved through an entrance into the next chamber. This chamber had a fire at the center with a natural hole up through the Earth for the smoke to exit. The ceilings were fairly low and the rock on the floor was smooth and warm. We took off our wraps and hung them to dry while we sat in a circle on the warm rock.

Calama said, "These are all women of the Dreamtime, Wise Women, and they each have a gift of wisdom from the Dreamtime for you."

I went to the first woman who was playing click sticks while someone else was playing a didjeridu. She was telling and showing me that rhythm and music are the road to the Dreamtime. Music carries you into the Dreamtime and supports the journey there.

She said, "You should learn more rhythms. Different rhythms will take you on different kinds of journeys. The music of different cultures will take you to different places. The didjeridu takes you very deep into the Dreamtime. You need to learn more of this."

The next woman had very white hair.

She said, "The Dreamtime vision allows you to find things. We use it to find water. The spirit of the water comes and points the way. To find things, one must call the spirit of that thing to you from the Dreamtime and it will show you. It might be food, plants, animals, water, warmth, or shelter. Listen and be receptive. The spirit of what you seek will appear and call you toward the place where you will find it."

I turned to the next woman who smiled and said, "When you use Dreamtime vision, use your left eye. Your right eye is dominant and is very much influenced by the physical world. Your left eye is more receptive to the Dreamtime and will activate your third eye or Dreamtime vision."

The fourth woman placed two sticks in my hands. They were paddle-shaped, with the paddle blade fitting into my hand and the other end coming to a long, straight point extending several inches beyond my fingers. I couldn't quite imagine what these sticks were for, but they felt very smooth and solid in my hands.

She said, "They have many uses. One is concentrating energy for healing work. Another is as antennae for receiving energy or signals from elsewhere. (Maybe dowsing?) A third is to pick things out of the Dreamtime. You will learn more about them as you use them."

Calama said, "These are enough gifts for today. I do not want to tax your memory. Sometimes experiences are difficult to bring back from the Dreamtime cave, so you need to go back and review what these gifts are."

I did that and had trouble remembering the second gift.

"What we forget is often what we most need to remember," said Calama.

Then I remembered the gift of finding things. The women began to play instruments and chant.

Calama said, "Dance these gifts, creating a story from them to help you remember."

I began dancing, using the music as my journey road, and then began to look for water and listen for its calling. I shifted my vision to my left eye, and I looked for water while using the sticks to receive the water's signals. When I pointed the sticks at the ground, two spots of light appeared on the ground as though they were flashlights shining a beam.

When I finished, Calama told me to come back and enter the cave the same way tomorrow. I asked how to get out of the cave, and she pointed out another doorway I could use to move outside this chamber. As I went through, I found myself on the opposite side of the mountain.

I called Cloud Dancer and we flew home.

*　　*　　*　　*　　*

I flew off, spotted the mountain, and landed by the entrance to the cave. I stepped into the cave and went over to the spiral slide. The splash into the warm water felt good. The other women were sitting around on the edge. It seemed as if the water itself was luminescent. The women moved into the water, and while we bathed, I was trying to figure out the source of the light. We then moved into the next chamber with the fire and warm rocks, hanging up our wraps and sitting in a circle around the fire.

Calama said, "We will continue with the gifts of wisdom. First, review the four gifts you have already received."

I did that as I walked by the women who gave them—music, finding, left eye, and sticks. I then sat before the fifth woman.

She said, "You need to place the Dreamtime image in your third eye and hold it there."

Up until this time, I was having great difficulty holding myself present—it was almost as though I was starting to fall asleep. I would drift off to some other place and then come back. I couldn't quite figure out what it meant to place the image in my third eye.

That area on my forehead began to tingle as I focused my attention there, and the woman repeated what she said before, "Place the Dreamtime image in your third eye. Move from your left eye to your third eye and then hold it there."

I tried this and it seemed to help a little to stay present, but I don't think I was getting the full meaning of it.

As I moved on to the next woman, she leaned forward and kissed me and said, "The Wise Woman within must become your lover."

I was surprised by her action and wasn't sure what she meant. I had images of my Wise Woman and myself as lovers, trying to comprehend the meaning. I asked her what that had to do with the Dreamtime.

She said, "Because she is the one who leads you. She has the wisdom to know the difference."

52

I contemplated that and saw how it was true. It was my wisdom which tells me where I am, what is real, what is possible. Loving her means becoming one with her and trusting her above all else.

Using images, the next woman told me that every possibility which exists in the Dreamtime can appear in physical reality. It is not likely, but possible, depending on what is being called forth by those present in a given time and space. I saw a dragon appearing and then disappearing as I thought about being on a walk in the woods.

"All is possible," she stated.

The eighth woman said, "The way you call things forth from the Dreamtime is with in-tension."

She said it as two words: "in tension."

"'In-tension' means inner tension which is created when you attach a line of energy to what you wish to bring forward. It is like a rubber band pulling it toward you."

I asked if it is like the times I think about the land and feel a tension pulling us together. [3]

"Yes, that is true. The Dreamtime is where it exists as a future possibility, and you are drawing it to you with in-tension."

Calama again asked me to review the gifts. When I did, I had difficulty remembering the second one. Third eye, Wise Woman lover, all possibilities, and in-tension. I then danced the story of picking up something from the Dreamtime and placing it in my third eye. Dancing with my Wise Woman lover, I looked at the possibilities from that place of wisdom, setting my in-tension to bring it forth.

Calama said we would do more next time. I left the cave and flew back.

---

[3] I had been working on acquiring land for a teaching center, and it seemed as though the land and I have some attachment.

*   *   *   *   *

I entered the cave and went down the spiral slide, noticing that it spiraled to the left. I splashed into the water, and the women were again waiting on the side of the pool. We bathed and moved into the adjacent chamber.

Calama said to review all the gifts I had received so far. I got a few—music, possibilities, left eye, sticks, finding things, loving the Wise Woman—but I could not remember the rest.

I then went on to the ninth woman, sitting in front of her and staring at her eyes as she stared back. I knew I was supposed to just look at her, and as I stared, her head transformed into an elephant's head. The others laughed and said they called her "the elephant" because of her incredible memory.

She said, "To remember things well and long, you need to picture them and attach a feeling. The gifts you remembered were the ones with which you had done that. It is important when traveling in the Dreamtime to take the time to do this so your memory will be vivid and lasting."

I thanked her for this gift.

The next woman said, "There is no darkness to be found in the Dreamtime which cannot be illuminated by the light you carry within you. There is no crevice within yourself which can stay dark when you shine your light upon it. There is nothing to fear from darkness."

I moved to the eleventh woman who said, "There are lines of light or energy which connect you to persons or objects in the physical world. These lines can be seen in the Dreamtime and followed to their source. This is what addictions are. They draw your energy and keep you attached. To get rid of them, you need to cut the lines. They may grow back if there is still feeling there, but just keep cutting them on a daily basis until they disappear. You can also use attachment lines to consciously connect you with what feeds you, that which promotes your growth. An example would be food addiction, where you cut the lines which lead you to the food which is not good for you and then consciously attach lines to healthy food."

Finally, the twelfth woman said, "Dreamtime can be used to get information for others. Each person, as well as every physical thing, has a representation in the Dreamtime. You can go and ask the Dreamtime representation what you can do to help. Any information given to you can be shared with the person. You should only do this if the person has requested your help."

I tried this, using a friend of mine.

I pictured him and asked what I could do to help and he said, "Nothing, unless I ask with honest desire to know."

I then turned back to Calama. She said I should review the four gifts, which I did—memory, light, lines, helping others.

She said, "I also have a gift for you, but I will give it to you in the sweat lodge which you have planned for tomorrow. The twelve women and I will be joining you. On the next trip, meet me back at the circle on the rock."

*   *   *   *   *

A friend had offered to be the fire-keeper for a solo sweat lodge for me. As we lit the fire, two red-tailed hawks circled, one quite low. I went up to the Medicine Wheel to smoke my pipe while the rocks were heated by the fire.

The first door was for working with the South energies for purification of my body and trust. I stared at the glowing rocks brought in for the West door and saw a bear. Shortly after that, the aboriginal women and Calama entered.

She said, "The gift I have for you is the gift of being fully conscious and aware of the Dreamtime in every moment. It is something which will unfold like a flower from a bud. You are the bud, and as you unfold you will see everything. The song you received before was for helping the bud to open and bloom. [4] You can call on us at anytime, not just during this learning time."

I asked about a friend of mine who was having some difficulty.

She said, "Your friend is like a flower that isn't sure it wants to bloom. The blossom opens sometimes at night like a desert flower but then folds tightly into a bud by day. She needs to learn to blossom in the day also."

During the North door, I saw a white buffalo in the large glowing rock, and I felt White Buffalo Woman present, standing over the fire pit. I told her I would use the pipe more if I felt I knew more about it.

She said, "Be patient. Teaching is on its way, as I also sit in the circle of Grandmothers. New teaching will be coming."

I felt that we were one and the same.

For the East door, I had my friend add one rock. It was very hot in the lodge by now, but it felt like one more rock wanted to be there. In the glowing rock, I saw the face of a Grandmother, and a rock that was placed there in the previous round began to glow again with another Grandmother face. The Grandmothers seemed to be saying that they will lead the way into the future, to trust them.

*   *   *   *   *

I met Calama at the circle on the red rock. I told her I was glad she had come in the sweat, and I understood that the Grandmothers would lead me. That was an important confirmation to me because of some opposition I felt at work yesterday for integrating spirituality into my teaching.

[4] While on a vision quest three years ago, I received a song from a balsam flower. The words are "Listen to our beauty song, We're calling you to sing along, Sing a song of Earth and Sky, Sing it loud and let it fly, When a beauty song is sung, we are one.

She said, "Walking the path of a Wise Woman in your time and culture is not easy, but it is your walk."

I said that I understood that.

"You need to get a flower to wear to represent my gift, as it is important to keep it in your awareness."

I was losing focus each time she spoke, drifting off to explore each of the scenes I was shown. I was thinking of a yellow flower because I like yellow roses, but she said the flower needed to be red as a symbol of the rocks here and the blood which connects all women.

"Focus is more important when many realities are available to you. Your focus is getting better. As you drift off, you remember to come back and can see the reason for being in the other reality—to show you an aspect of what we were talking about. With time, you will be able to stay even more focused on where you are at the same time. I will leave you here alone in the circle and you may leave when you are ready. Tomorrow we will meet in ceremony. You need to review the lessons of the Dreamtime and you will be more rested then."

As I lay down in the circle, I could see and hear thunderclouds gathering, and it became very dark. I drifted a little but I am not sure where. Then I got up and mounted Cloud Dancer and we flew home through the thunderclouds.

* * * * *

I reviewed what I had learned from Calama and the other aboriginal women and then flew off to the red rock.

Calama was waiting there. She asked me to sit in the circle to look into the Dreamtime to see what symbol I would carve in the rock. Instantly, I saw a symbol and said I already knew. She said I only knew part of it and that I was to sit in the circle to see the rest of the symbol while the women prepared for the ceremony. She said she would be back shortly.

I sat there and saw the symbol of a reverse spiral. I looked carefully to be sure it was spiraling to the left. It was a flower and had a stem on it. As I continued to look, I saw that it also had twelve petals which represented the twelve gifts. There was also a partial reverse swastika around it which was an indication that the teaching was given by a Grandmother of the wind.

Calama came to get me and led me down the path where the symbols are carved in the stone. She gave me a diamond which I used to carve the symbol on the rock. What I realized as I walked by the other symbols is that when I looked at them, it was like seeing a video of the teaching they represented. I was anxious to see if my symbol would be the same. I looked at it when I was done and it was. When I looked at it, using the Dreamtime vision, I could see the teaching as though it was happening all over again.

Calama came up to me and said, "I see you have discovered how to read the symbols. Look at this one and see what it means."

I looked and saw a snake. Then there was an image of a person being eaten by the snake and becoming the snake. I told Calama that this woman had been eaten by a snake, had become the snake, and had the powers and gifts of knowing how to shed skin.

She smiled and showed me another symbol. I saw a large bird pick up a woman and carry her to a nest where the bird fed her and taught her its wisdom.

She just smiled and said, "The women are waiting."

We went past the circle to a more secluded spot. The women had a fire going and were playing click sticks, didjeridus, and other instruments. They said I should dance and listen for my song.

I started to dance. With my right arm out, I turned to the left, gathering the past. With my left arm out, I turned to the right to move into the future. Then I drew from all that is inside and opened up to all that is outside through many dimensions. Opening like a flower to the Dreamtime. I open like a flower to the Dreamtime.

I was just getting into this when Pooh Bear woke up and started chasing another dog who was visiting. I wanted to stay longer but I knew that I couldn't. Calama said that I could think of the dance before I went to sleep and came back here.

I wanted to give the women something. I went to each one, thanked her for her gift (which I remembered) and gave her a crystal. I thanked Calama, and she said I should come to the tipi tomorrow and that I would need to have the song and dance complete by then.

That evening I put on some didjeridu music, and the song and dance came:

All that has ever been (right arm out turning left)
All that will ever be (left arm out turning right)
All that is living within me (both arms up the body
   to the heart)
I open up to all that is (continue up above head)
I open like a flower to the Dreamtime (arms opening out)
I open like a flower to the Dreamtime (arms opening out).

*   *   *   *   *

I went to the tipi, knocked, and went in. I sat by the door while Mariah spoke.

"We are here to complete your Dreamtime journey. Tomorrow you will meet our representative from China. Now that your time is freer, we would like you to continue to journey five days a week. It might be more convenient for your days off to be on the weekend, but we'll leave that up to you. Learning the wisdom is important, but practicing it every day in all that you do is what makes you wise. You must become more aware of the applications to your everyday living. You also need to write five days a week. This will help you integrate."

I looked at Calama and she was smiling at me. Akama also was, but for some reason I couldn't remember her name. She said it was alright, since my brain was preoccupied with the Dreamtime.

The women began to play their instruments with Calama on the didjeridu. I began to dance and sing the song. The last part of the dance changed as I thought it might, to turning first to the left, opening my arms like a flower petal, then turning to the right, doing the same.

After I danced for a while, Mariah called me over. Calama and Akama assisted her. Mariah asked me to lie down and then reached into my third eye and took out a small crystal. It was the one I had discovered a number of years ago while meditating. She replaced it with a very large, clear crystal. They all then placed their hands over my forehead and sent energy to activate the crystal they had placed there. It was somehow opening me up to the Dreamtime.

I then went back to dancing. After that, I finally left, coming back to my living room to continue dancing in this reality.

3

The Energy Flow

When I went to the tipi, Mariah called me over to her, and I greeted Akama and Calama on the way. Mariah then introduced me to Che li lan from the Northwest mountain area of China. Mariah said I would be spending the next two weeks with Che li lan learning more wisdom. Che li lan has gray hair which was twisted around her head like a beehive. She was dressed in beautiful garments of red silk.

We started to leave through the top of the tipi, and I asked whether she might like to go on my horse so I wouldn't have to come back for him. She thought that was a good idea, so we both climbed on Cloud Dancer and flew off to her land. The snow-covered mountains were majestic in the distance. We landed in a meadow quite high up near where a waterfall dropped over the side of a cliff into a deep gorge.

She said, "This is the high plain country which is the summer home of my people. We stay here where the sheep and goats have grass, and we grow small gardens from seeds we save. The wild plants in the meadows and ravines also feed us. My silk dress is from trading with others and is for ceremony. Normally we dress in more plain, woven woolen garments."

All of this information was, of course, in answer to my questioning mind. The homes seemed to be constructed of hide and wood and were round—sort of like a yurt. Che li lan invited me into her home, and we sat on short, wooden stools with pillows on them and drank green tea. I asked of the role of women in her community.

She said, "I was just about to tell you about that. As I have heard from the other Grandmothers, you have many questions. The women here do much of the work but also have much of the power. Men and women work together on many tasks, but we differ in role when it comes to other matters.

"Women are carriers of the Earth energy and it is our responsibility to nurture the flow. By that I mean the flow of energy in nature and between humans and nature—like harmony. We have the ability to see where the flow has been disrupted and can see how a block can be removed, which often requires letting go of something.

"The men are formal ceremonialists, and they then create the ritual for the removal of the block to restore the flow. They depend on us to see the flow and the disturbance, and we depend on them to create the ritual for its removal.

"As women, we must nurture this flow within and between all things to create overall harmony. Nurturing means feeding something so it will grow, but also knowing when things need to be let go."

I asked how women learned this.

"It is natural to all women, but it needs to be encouraged in young girls. They are very excited about developing their abilities. It is our responsibility as wisdom women to teach them and help them to use this talent for the good of their people and Earth. But you will have more opportunity to learn about this later."

I asked if her name had a meaning and she said it means "flows through it." I thanked her and turned to get my horse.

She admired him and said, "Come here tomorrow. You will recognize this place by the falls. It is unique in this area."

64

*　　*　　*　　*　　*

When I flew off to meet Che li lan, the falls could be seen from quite far away. This is such a beautiful country. A rainbow appeared in the mist from the falls.

Che li lan invited me to come in and have tea. She had on woolen pants and a shawl and asked me if I wanted some woolen clothing. Even though the Sun was shining, it was a very cool morning at that elevation. I said I did not like wool next to my skin, and she said I could put the shawl and pants, which were narrow at the ankles and baggy otherwise, over my other clothes. We sat in her home and had tea while she talked.

"Yesterday we spoke of nurturing the flow. Everything is always in motion, since even the rocks beneath us vibrate with energy. That energy is in constant motion, flowing through us and through everything around us. When the flow stops—what you might call a block—disease develops. Many healing techniques which have been developed center around getting the energy moving again. The moving energy, or the flow, is a state of balance. Let's go out and walk around to see this in action."

We walked out among the homes and came upon a mother with a small child who was sick.

Che li lan said, "This child has become attached to an object which another child has and he does not have. It has caused a block in his energy flow. A ritual will be done for him which will not only move the energy, but teach him about how attachment keeps us from allowing the energy to move through us.

"Quite often attachment is the source of a blocked flow. It would be like moving freely with the current of a river and then grabbing on to something outside yourself. This action would keep you from moving freely with the energy, and you would be battered by the waters of your emotions as they try to free you up again. Nurturing the flow within us and detecting attachments and potential blocks early is part of the awareness which the Wise Woman develops."

What about the flow between people and nature of which you spoke?

"All of nature, including ourselves, is set up based on cycles of energy. When we honor these cycles, we move with and nurture the flow. The falls and river here are a good reminder to us of these cycles. The water pours over the falls every day, but where does the water go and where does it come from? It goes through the land to the ocean, feeding many on its way. In the ocean and along the way, it rises to form clouds. The clouds go over the mountains to drop rain and snow, and the water comes together again to form this river. And the cycle continues.

"Yes," she said, reading my questioning mind, "it is a counterclockwise motion, because the waters of Earth are governed by the Moon. When we give our energy to the plants and the animals in the form of love, they give back to our spirits and our bodies in companionship, teachings, and food. Our bodies cycle the food into energy which can be given back to the Earth and plants to use again.

"Our children have a relationship with what they eat and are taught that this is part of the energy exchange cycle which keeps them in balance and healthy. Tomorrow we will be looking at the flow within you and between you and all that is around you."

An older man walked over to us, and Che li lan introduced him as an elder of the community who performs ritual to maintain the flow. I said I could see why she was given her name. She truly was the energy which flows through her body.

*   *   *   *   *

Again I went off to Che li lan's. When I got there, I was looking at the terrain, wondering where their winter camp was. She said that it was down in the valley where the river and land at the bottom widen out.

She invited me in for tea and introduced me to four other women who, like herself, were Wise Women. We were all sitting around in a circle. I was trying to figure out what it was we were

66

sitting around. It seemed like a fire of some sort—I am having a very difficult time focusing today. I feel as though I'm drifting off all the time, almost falling asleep.

Che li lan said that she and the other women were going to be looking at the flow of energy within me.

"Each of us uses a different method of accessing this flow. I use feeling."

Without touching me, she moved her hands over my body.

"The crystal is not fully activated yet and is creating some difficulties for you. You tense the muscles in your face in resistance, and the muscle tension blocks the flow of energy. You must keep them relaxed at all times."

She seemed to be sending some energy to the crystal.

The next woman said, "I work by seeing colors and can determine the flow of energy that way. I see the block in your head and neck area by the difference in color."

Another woman said, "I can see the lines of light through which energy flows to and from your body. You have lines still attached to food and have many other attachments to physical things which your energy flows to. You need to cut the ones which are not bringing energy back to you in some way."

The following woman assessed the energy flow by listening. She listened to my body and the movement of energy when I walked. She said it sounded nice when I walked.

The last one also used vision but saw pictures instead of colors. I couldn't quite get what she saw, but there were some mandalas which came into my mind. I don't know how they were related.

I told Che li lan that I was sorry that I was so unfocused and kept drifting off. She said it was okay and that we would work on it more tomorrow. I went out, got on my horse and flew back, feeling very groggy and spacey.

*　*　*　*　*

I was so spacey all day yesterday. I ended up going to the mall after a relatively healthy day of eating and had a hot fudge sundae and a pretzel. I felt much better afterward but am paying for it today. I feel just as spacey today as yesterday, but toxic also. I become aware of what I am doing—trying to ground the energy by slowing my vibrational rate. I need to find a more productive way of handling this energy.

I went to meet Che li lan and told her I was sorry that I was unfocused during my visits with her.

She said, "All is as it should be. I am teaching you about energy flow and blocks. You have a block in the sixth chakra and it is creating physical discomfort. Your eating is an attempt to slow the flow at lower levels. Come in and we will do some work on this block."

The other women were in her home and they began to work on me. It felt as though they were reaching inside my head and wiping off the large crystal in my third eye. It felt good when they did that. They were talking about how it was not fully functioning yet and that the flow of energy was being backed up. I asked what frequency the crystal was tuned to and got an image of it receiving and sending vibrations to various parts of my body as well as receiving through my third eye.

Che li lan said, "You must not try to slow the flow by eating. You might be uncomfortable for a few days, but the energy will make it work better. You might take some herbs for the physical condition this block has caused, and it would be good to make the special tea which has been given to you. That will help.[1]

"I know you are anxious to go to the place by the waterfall you have had glimpses of, but we will wait until tomorrow for that. Today we will go to the elder I introduced you to before, and he will do ritual around this block."

---

[1] A friend had given me a Manchurian mushroom to make a special tea which is said to be very nourishing to the body.

We all went outside and found this man. His name is Kol tat. In a sunny spot, all the women sat in a circle, and I lay on the ground in the center. Kol tat began chanting and making movements with his hands over me. The women picked up the chant and duplicated his movement. It seemed as though they were moving the energy with flowing movements. Their arms reached toward the Sun, bringing that energy down, and then pulled up the Earth energy from the ground. He opened energy holes in the bottom of my feet, at my crown chakra, and at my third eye.

While he was still moving the energy, I could see the crystal at my third eye begin to spin as a turbine does with the flow of water. My head felt somewhat better. I thanked Kol tat and Che li lan and headed off to find Cloud Dancer.

*   *   *   *   *

Feeling much better today after the energy work last time.

When I saw Che li lan waiting near the waterfall, I thanked her for the work she did last time.

She said, "The crystal isn't spinning fully yet, but is much better. You might try spinning again but not so many times—maybe fifteen to allow your body to catch up." [2]

I told her that I would make the tea today.

"Good. It will be ready before we finish our work. Today we are going to the women's spot by the falls. Stop trying to picture it before you get there. Some things cannot be imagined before

---

[2] I had been spinning thirty-three times each day as part of my morning exercise but had stopped when I became very nauseous during my journey with Calama.

they are experienced. The other women are already there. It is such a beautiful day for a walk."

In the sparkling sunlight, we started down a trail that zigzagged back and forth along the waterfall. I kept looking to find a nice sunny spot with grass near the water, but it wasn't there. We came to a point where there was an opening in the rock near the waterfall and went in. A cave? This is not at all what I thought it would be. We moved through the darkness in a tunnel traveling upward until we came out in a chamber with sunlight shining down through a small hole in the ceiling onto an amethyst crystal in the center of the chamber. My eyes were still adapting to the dimly lit room. There was the sound of water rushing as though the river was close and almost over us.

As my eyes adjusted, I saw the other women sitting around, and then I looked up and it was as though we were in an enormous amethyst geode. The whole ceiling was amethyst crystals. Then I realized that I was sitting on smoothly polished, purple crystal. The hue in the chamber was one of purple light. The amount of energy in the chamber was amazing!

Che li lan said, "This is where women come to learn about the flow and their special talents. Each of us has learned to use our own special way of 'seeing' the flow. We ask you to join us in our continued learning while you focus on finding your unique way of seeing. It may be related to the dream you had last night.[3]

---

[3] In the dream, I was with a group of people and we were looking at a refrigerator. There was a woman trapped inside, not as though she was in the refrigerator, but part of it. I could not see her, but I knew she was there. I also knew that it was the steady beat that the refrigerator's motor made that drew her to it and kept her there. I knew that what was needed to get her out was a beat that was polyrhythmic. I gathered everyone around, and when I looked at the refrigerator again, I could etherically see the woman in the refrigerator. I told everyone that they needed to pick up a different beat or rhythm and keep it up until she came out.

"The beginning point in 'seeing' is to be able to experience the flow within your own being. Focus on the Grandmother crystal at the center and see what she teaches you."

The women began a chant, almost like toning, which filled the cave. I was trying to understand the syllables, but I couldn't quite get it. I focused on the crystal and on my own flow and could feel the energy moving through me.

Che li lan said, "If you scan your own energy on a daily basis, you will never have sickness because you will see the blocks as they begin to form and will take action to remove them. It is not easy to learn to see the energy. You need to practice as you are moving throughout your day. We will do more with this next time."

It was taking me a while just to be in that much energy and stay focused. I headed out of the cave and climbed back up to where Cloud Dancer was waiting.

I know I need to do some grounding activities today—perhaps working in my garden will help.

*   *   *   *   *

I met Che li ln at the waterfall, and she said we would be going back to the crystal cave again. We went down the pathway and entered the cave. The women were already there, and some kind of candles had been placed around the sides of the chamber, creating a soft light and warmth. Che li lan spoke.

"You must continue to see the energy patterns in yourself before you can become familiar with your way of 'seeing.' Try to step outside your body and look at it to see the energy."

I tried this and found it extremely difficult to see myself. I was also finding it very difficult to stay focused in general because I did not get enough sleep last night. At one point, I could clearly see the energy moving up my left leg to the top of my head and down my right side. This was about the only clarity I got. I told Che li lan that I was sorry that I kept drifting off.

She said it was all part of learning what I need to do. She suggested that I visualize looking at myself in a mirror. I had done that before, but even that was difficult at the moment.

Che li lan said, "Practice more during the day and we will continue tomorrow."

I left the cave, went up to where my horse was waiting, and flew back.

*   *   *   *   *

I felt more alert today. Che li lan said we would go back to the crystal cave. I told her I was having a lot of difficulty with this lesson, and she just said we would continue to work on it.

In the cave, she asked me to stare at my reflection in the crystal in the center. I did that but kept getting pictures of flowers and other stuff as though my mind was trying to decide what to see. I said to myself: I can't do this.

Che li lan asked me to stay positive. I knew that was important, so I dropped the self-doubt and tried again.

She said to come over to a wall which looked like polished crystal. I stood facing my image and began to see. First, I could see the same pattern I had seen before—the energy flowed in the bottom of my left foot, up my left side, over the top of my head, and down my right side. It seemed to be flowing smoothly.

Then I saw the energy flow in my left hand, up my arm, across my chest, and out my right arm and hand. That also was flowing smoothly. Energy also came in the tailbone/pubic bone area and up through my chakras. At first I saw a slowing down at my third eye, but I felt that I was seeing that because I knew there was a problem there. So I refocused and scanned that flow again.

This time it seemed as though the neck area—the thyroid—was sticky and not spinning correctly. I cut loose some strands of something which was slowing it down and saw it spin faster and faster around the thyroid. As I did this, a feeling of energy came into my body.

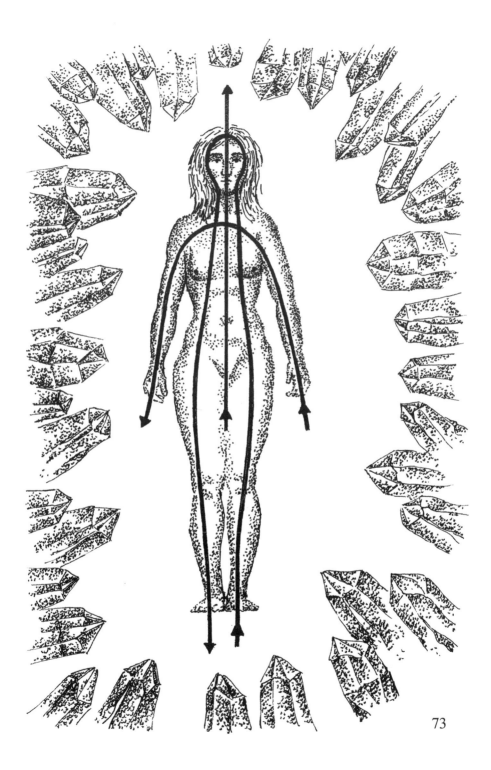

73

I then moved up to the third eye, pituitary level. Things were also still sluggish there, as though the pituitary was being overworked. Again, I cleared away strands which held the crystal from spinning, and it began to spin faster. The flow seemed to be smooth now. I looked at Che li lan.

She said, "You must scan these flows in your body daily and make adjustments to prevent illness. Now you must try this on others to see if you can see their flow."

I asked if a friend who was not feeling well could come here. Che li lan said yes and I called my friend in by seeing her there in the cave with us. I had already told her earlier in the day that I would do a healing meditation for her.

She stood and I began to scan the flow in her body. I followed it up her left leg to the top of her head and down the right side. There was something interrupting the flow at the top of her head, like a knot or break in the line. This resulted in a decreased flow down her right side and a stopped-up flow on the left. I worked on the knot, smoothing it out until the flow was more even. Then I looked at the left-arm-to-right-arm flow. There did not seem to be much coming into the left arm. Then I noticed that her fist was clenched. I asked her to open up her left hand and be receptive to the flow through her. That solved the problem.

When I looked at the flow through the chakras, the block was in the solar plexus. There was something stuck there which looked like a gear or wheel with notches. It was as if it rusted in place, seized up. I dropped some oil on it and it began to turn. I gave it a strong spin and it really began to move. The upper chakras were fine but had not been functioning well because of the block in the solar plexus. Once that began to move, the flow was restored to the other chakras. I then asked Che li lan how my friend could learn to heal herself.

She said, "She can come and we will teach her if she wants, but she has many other teachers. She needs to raise her vibrational rate in order to heal herself. If the healing occurs when her body is at a higher vibrational rate, then the changes made will continue even if she drops back to a lower rate."

I thanked Che li lan. She said to come back tomorrow and we would work some more. I left the cave and climbed up to my horse. Kol tat was there and I waved.

He said, "See you tomorrow."

* * * * *

I met Che li lan near her home and we went in to have tea and to talk.

She said, "The method of seeing the flow which you have found is unique to you. Others will experience it differently, so that it is not something you can teach to someone else—you can only help them to find their own way of seeing."

But what do you do when you see the image which is blocking the flow? How can the person you are working with know what is there if they can't use this method? And if you have different people using different methods looking at the same individual, won't they find different things?

"What you see as the block is symbolic of the issue or problem. Your job is to see, not to interpret. The interpretation is left up to the person. While different people will see different symbols, and their methods of finding the blocks differ, they will always come up with the same area, and symbols will have similar meanings. We need to talk a little more about how the rest of the process goes. Once you have found the symbols of the blocks and shared them with the individual, you ask that person to tune into that area of the body and those symbols to get more information on what the block is about.

"If you are working on yourself, then all parts of this process can be done by you. We encourage as much of the process as possible to be done by the individual. They will then identify the cause of this block and say what needs to be done to remove it. If they are ready to have it removed, then a ritual is done which focuses energy on that area while the individual visualizes whatever process is needed to remove the block. Let's go to the healing lodge to get some experience with this process."

We went to another lodge in the village where there were several waiting to be treated. Some of the other women and Kol tat were also there. The first woman came forward, and Che li lan asked me to look for blocks to the flow in her body.

As I scanned the three flows, the only one which seemed odd was the left to right flow. When the flow went through the heart area, it seemed to break into many smaller streams which had much less force. I described this to the woman and asked her to look in the heart area to see what was there.

She said that there were holes in her heart which were created by sadness. The holes were made by losses—she lost a child to sickness and her husband to accident and her belongings in a fire. I asked her what needed to happen to correct this flow. She said that the holes must heal over. I asked if she was ready at this time to heal them and she said she was.

She then lay down and Kol tat asked her to concentrate on seeing those holes heal over and close while he focused energy on the heart area. She seemed much lighter afterward.

Che li lan said, "You can see that the individual is asked to fully participate in the healing process and is given full responsibility for determining where the block came from and what should be done about it. Let's try again."

A man walked over, and as I began to scan his flow, I detected a problem with the up-and-down flow in the hip area, mostly on the left. The left-right flow was fine, but the chakra flow was disrupted in the belly. I looked closer to get a symbol of the block. It seemed as though there was a hole there, quite large, that I could actually see through. It was large enough that it was disrupting the up-down flow at that level also. I described to him what I saw and asked him to focus on his belly and see what this was about.

He said that he had been very hurt by something someone said, and he became angry instead of expressing how he felt—he had been denying his hurt feelings. I asked him what needed to happen and he said he must close the hole and feel those feelings. I asked if he felt ready to do that and he said he did.

Kol tat asked him to lie down and visualize the hole closing while allowing himself to feel the hurt as energy was focused on his belly. After some moments, the man began to weep as the hurt was released. Afterwards his flow was restored to normal and he felt much better.

Che li lan said that we would meet at her house again tomorrow and talk some more about this process.

*   *   *   *   *

I met Che li lan by her home and we went in for tea. I told her I was impressed with the healing system she taught me. I assume that the information that I get from scanning a person's body is something which I would share only if they ask for my help.

She said, "That is generally true, but in some cases, if you have information, you can ask the person if they would like it."

I began thinking about a person's body I had scanned for practice. I saw that in the chakra flow at the heart level, the energy scattered and only one small stream continued to the higher chakras. I thought about this in relation to that person needing to work on unconditional love issues of both self and others, and it began to make sense. Of course, that is only my interpretation. I did not share the information.

"Many times, if people don't ask for your help, they are simply not ready to work on those issues, and readiness is always necessary for healing. You also must realize that the symbols you see are of the emotional issues which have either produced or are in the process of producing a physical problem. If no physical condition exists yet, you are working on a preventative level. If there is a physical condition, the body will usually need to be supported with other physical methods—tonics, herbs, massage, and so on—once the emotional block is removed.

"You are also not directly seeing the spiritual component, although it is certainly related to the emotional one. That you will learn from another teacher. There may be karmic causes for certain emotional blocks that might be important to determine."

What about the system you have where the men do the ritual and the women see? Does it need to be that way?

"No, this is only the division which we have developed which works in our community. A woman can learn to focus energy in ritual just as a man can learn to see. You will learn about focusing energy from another teacher. We do not teach this here because it is a skill which belongs to our men. It is often useful when you come into healing groups to divide up the work, since some of you will be better at seeing and others at focusing energy. The healing process is accelerated when there are more people sending energy or concentrating it, as you observed the women doing by sitting in circle during the ritual and chanting.

"While healing can be done on your own, it is much quicker when several are present. If you are working alone, it is good to open up to the white light to energize the process. You have learned well, and tomorrow we will conclude our teachings here with a ceremony in the crystal cave."

Is there anything special I need to bring or wear?

"Amethyst would be good. We will have clothing for you."

I thanked her and said I would miss coming to this beautiful place. She said I can always return for a visit.

*　　*　　*　　*　　*

I found an amethyst crystal given to me by a friend. It reminds me of the polished wall where I saw my energy flow. Before I journeyed, I used breathing to move the flow within me: breathing in my left hand to the heart and breathing out of my heart to my right hand; breathing in up my left side to the top of my head and breathing out down my right side; breathing in up through the chakras to the heart level and breathing out from the heart chakra to the crown chakra. It felt good.

I met Che li lan near her home and we went inside so I could dress. She gave me a red skirt slit up each side and a black top with a high collar and buttons. Both the skirt and top were silk.

She gave me boots of some kind, also of a silky material. She did my hair in rolls on either side, with the rolls held up with a pin through them.

We headed for the crystal cave and she said the other women were already there and had warmed it up. I asked how they did that, and she said it was through raising the vibration in the crystal so it hummed. That produced warmth.

I went in and could feel the hum and vibration. I knew I was to move with it in a receptive way. When I did that, the words to a song began to form:

> I move with the flow of the Earth and Sky,
> The flow that moves through my being.
> I call on the purple crystal light
> To show me the symbols for my healing.

This continued for some time and then Che li lan said, "You have learned well and must remember to practice seeing the flow. Breathing is a good way to energize the flow. You will learn more on other journeys which will be used along with this method. Next time, we will meet back in the tipi."

I thanked Che li lan for her patience in teaching me and thanked the other women for sharing their gifts with me. I gave them each a crystal. Che li lan said Kol tat was up by my horse waiting to say goodbye.

I left the cave, found Kol tat, and thanked him for his willingness to share with me. As he gave me a boost onto Cloud Dancer, he said we would meet again.

*　　*　　*　　*　　*

When I got off Cloud Dancer I fell again—I think this must be a cue to get centered. I took a moment to center myself and felt a little better.

I had on the clothes I wore for the ceremony last time. When I entered the tipi, I sat on a fur by the door and acknowledged each of the women.

Mariah began to speak. "This has been a difficult journey for you."

Yes, I said, I seem to be having a lot of physical adjustments to make.

"Part of you doubts the validity of the healing methods you are being taught."

Yes, a small part of me doubts, but the larger part knows that these healing methods are real and correct.

"Doubting can be useful when it is used to discern the validity of outer knowledge, but it is not useful when it is directed at the knowledge which comes from within. Doubting slows the process and reduces the power of the inner knowing. You need to learn to use doubt as a tool of your left brain which you can direct at will."

Yes, I can see that, but I am not sure how to turn it off when I don't want it there.

"You are learning. That is part of the wisdom you will acquire. Your doubt is part of the conflict seen in the throat chakra. When it is cleared, you will have more energy. Perhaps it is also a question of Two Feathers Shining Brightly taking direction from Blue Moon Bear without question." [4]

---

[4] A couple of years ago, when I was working on male/female balance, my inner female became known to me as Blue Moon Bear, a warrior woman with great wisdom, strength, and gentleness. My inner male was known as Two Feathers Shining Brightly. My inner male was very capable of creating things in the physical world. My inner female and male developed a harmonious relationship in which she set the agenda and he carried it out.

80

I'm not sure that's it. I see him as very supportive of her.

"His job is to question outer information, not that from her inner knowing. We want you to sing and dance your song while you free yourself from doubt."

As I sang and danced, I felt the purple light moving through me. When I sang the first line, "I move with the flow of the Earth and Sky," I bent over and moved my hands up the left side of my body, over the top of my head, and down the right side. With the second line, "The flow that moves through my being," my right hand crossed over to my left arm which was out to the side. I drew my right hand to my heart and then stretched it out to the right while my left hand followed through my heart and out to the right hand. My hands moved up my chakras on the next line, "I call on the purple crystal light." On the last line, "To show me the symbols for my healing," my hands came back down the chakras, crossing like intertwined snakes. I could feel my throat and third eye chakras spinning faster. When I was done, I felt as though I was glowing with purple light.

Mariah again cut the strings, slowing down the crystal in my third eye. She said to use the purple light as a lubricant for the crystal to keep it spinning faster. When I did that, it started spinning very fast, and I felt much better.

I thanked them all and told them how important their teachings were to me and how committed I was to sharing them.

She said, "That is why we chose you. Tomorrow you will be traveling with our representative from Machu Picchu, so be sure you are rested so you can focus well."

I thanked them again and left the tipi to fly back home.

4

Dreaming Women

I went to the tipi, more centered but not as rested as I'd like to have been. Mariah introduced me to the woman from Machu Picchu. Her hair was black with strands of silver and she was not as old as some of the others. I tried to get her name but had a lot of difficulty. I think it is Mazra.

We both got on Cloud Dancer and headed to Peru. She pointed out a very tall, white mountain peak in the Andes and said to follow the river gorge from there and it would lead to Machu Picchu. Since I have been there before, it was not difficult to spot from the air. We landed on an upper level by the large stone with the ring carved in it. The terraces were very beautiful, with all kinds of plants in flower.

As we walked down toward her hut, we passed many women, each dressed in a very simple, off-white dress of woven material, maybe cotton. Mazra gave me a dress to wear which was made from this very soft material.

She said, "This is a time when there are mostly women living here, and the purpose is to train young girls both in working with plants and with energy. The most knowledgeable older women live here and continue their experimental work with plants as well as preparing for occasional visits from Sky Beings. Young girls who wish to train as healers, teachers, and plant workers are sent here to learn from the elders. You will be learning some of what we teach them about working with energy. We will begin tomorrow."

I went to my horse and flew home, feeling very sleepy.

*   *   *   *   *

It is the first day of moontime today, so no wonder I was so tired yesterday.

As I flew off to meet Mazra, I saw the tall, white mountain and followed the river gorge, landing at Machu Picchu.

Mazra said that since I was in moontime I should wear a red dress and follow her to the temple of the Moon. We walked up a hill with terraces of flowers and herbs. She said they were herbs and foods which nourish the Moon woman. We continued up to the stone structure which had an inner room that seemed round in comparison to the angular structure of the other buildings. It had a thatched roof with a round hole in the center. She told me that I should stay there by myself, because this is a time to connect with the inner teacher.

I sat down on a bench which was carved into the stone. It had woven mats on it and a blanket. As I sat there, I began to look around and see the room in more detail. In all directions there were window-like openings through which you could look and see over the mountains and valley. Clouds and mist seemed to hang around some of the higher mountaintops. There were shelves in the stone walls which held carvings with many colors of inlaid stone.

Before she left, Mazra gave me a meditation piece. She said the one I received when I was at Machu Picchu before would be used at another time. The piece she gave me was circular, flat, and smooth, with a space near the top carved to look like a Moon. It was red stone and felt very wonderful.

In the window, there were flowers in a pot. The whole place felt so feminine and beautiful! I had chills running over my body

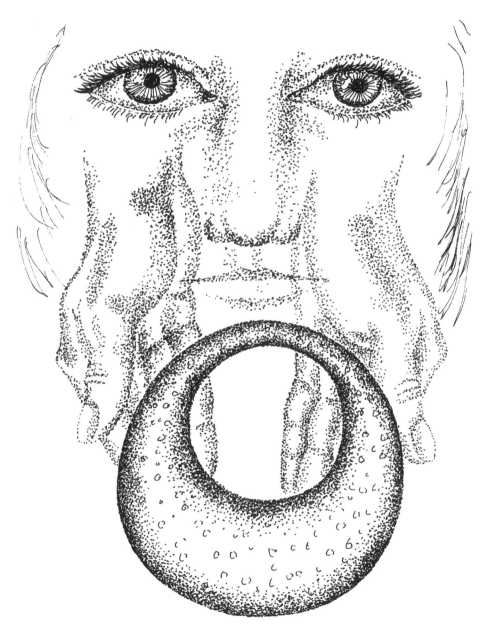

85

the whole time I was there. There was a clear crystal in the center of the room under the round hole in the roof. When the Sun came through and shined on it, the room filled with rainbows. Just then a large bird flew in and perched in the window.

I tried to determine what kind of bird it was and clearly saw an eagle. I lost focus a little and when I came back, the eagle was still there. It had something in its talons. It was an empty turtle shell.

I walked over to it, and the eagle said, "This turtle has fed my babies, and I offer its shell to you for a pouch in which you can keep special things."

I couldn't quite get what I was to keep in it, but it was clear that I should decorate it and use it. The eagle said that she was a female. Then she put her head and beak into my throat chakra and placed a crystal there. I couldn't figure out what color it was. At first I thought it was blue, then green, then red, then black, then clear.

She said, "These stones of many colors are for your male Eagle in your throat chakra. He has been waiting for them. They will make your voice strong and flexible with the many colors to choose from. They will help in bringing back the feminine voice to your world."

She also seemed to be connecting with my Eagle by touching beaks.

I thanked her and she said, "We will meet again," and flew off.

Mazra came back to get me and said I would have a chance to spend more time there later. I could not believe how incredibly beautiful the place was. She led me back down to the main area and said we would go to work tomorrow.

*　　*　　*　　*　　*

I met Mazra on the flat area up high.

She said, "I want to give you a tour today to let you know what we will be working with. One of the functions of the women who live here is to move through each day in ceremony as a way of being in harmony with the life around us. We gather each morning at sunrise to honor all that the light and warmth of the Sun Being brings each day. We also maintain good relationship with the waters and clouds to be able to call in the rains if needed. And so it is throughout our day—one long ceremony of being in good relationship and honoring the beauty around us. Some of the women here specialize as plant workers."

We were now walking among very beautiful terraced gardens where many women moved among the plants.

"The plant workers spend a portion of each day in meditation with the plants, sharing their love with them and learning from them. It is during this time that the knowledge of how to better care for the plants comes as well as the methods of developing new varieties. The new seeds which are developed here are taken out to the surrounding villages, and the people there are taught how to work with the plants. Some of the plant workers stay here all the time, while others become the travelers to carry the new seeds and teachings to the people.

"Some of these women also specialize in the preparation of the plants for food, again done in ceremony and in communication with the plant regarding the best time to harvest it and the best way to prepare it to retain nutrients and flavor. These women are also the ones who have the knowledge of plants used for healing."

Are all the women here vegetarians?

"Yes. The plants provide us with all the nutrients we need for the work we do. The people in villages are not vegetarians entirely. We maintain a good relationship with the animals in the surrounding area. Animals are not kept as pets here, but the ones who live around us often come to visit and teach us, because they know we will not try to hurt or capture them.

"Another specialty which some of the women here have developed has to do with energy systems. These are general energy exchanges within and around Earth. Magnetic energy lines, vortexes, and portals are some of what these women study. You have already learned about some of the energy flow within humans, and this moves a step beyond. These are dreaming women who monitor the more general energy systems of Earth and the changes which are occurring. They also are the women who communicate with the Sky Beings. You will be learning from both of these groups of women while you are here. We will begin next time with the plant workers."

I said I would see her tomorrow. I flew back home on Cloud Dancer.

*   *   *   *   *

I waited for Mazra on the high area, enjoying the beautiful day. She took me down to the terraces where women were working. I sat there and was shown different things. I saw how gently the women worked with the plants. Then I saw a very large black panther come walking through. No one seemed surprised. He walked over to one woman who fed him some plants.

Mazra said, "We always try to grow enough for our animal friends. Of course, we then ask that they stay out of our supplies."

I saw a picture of an underground vault of tightly-fitted stone. The stone at the bottom of the doorway was smooth and larger at the top than the bottom. This made it difficult for critters to enter.

Then Mazra said, "I want you to sit with this plant for a while and see what it has to say."

I sat in front of a plant which had a very beautiful and delicate flower, light pink with darker pink stripes and broad flat leaves, about two feet tall. I was admiring its beauty when it began to speak.

"It is when you see my beauty and send me love that the lines of communication open."

I said they must be open then, because you are beautiful.

"They are open from me too, because I also see your beauty and send you love.

"Plants have much to teach humans. We can tell you how we might change to produce larger or different tasting fruit, and when we guide the change it will always be in balance with all that is around us. When humans try to do this on their own, the result is often out of balance. Plants willingly give of ourselves for food, as we understand that our essence is never changed but only released by the process. This essence then enters the forming seeds of other plants of our kind. So it is also when human bodies give up their physical form. Their essence is unchanged and continues the journey.

"When you use us for food, it is important, as you know, to be aware of the transformation you are creating—using the nutrients and releasing the essence. It is the essence which can be healing on emotional levels before it moves back to seed. Any plant can tell you of its food or medicinal characteristics for humans or animals. For instance, my flower will become an edible fruit. My leaves can be used for a medicinal tea for congestion, and my roots are a strong tonic for the digestive system.

"Plants will not, however, talk to just anyone. We only speak to those who have a desire to learn and use what we teach. If you sat down here with the intention of just seeing whether a plant can communicate, I would not waste my time speaking with you. You instead sat with the intention to learn, and so I share. This is the time of your life when speaking to plants should be an everyday occurrence, because we have much wisdom to share about balance in your world and in your body."

Perhaps you could come with me and grow in my garden.

"I do not believe I would fit in that ecosystem but my kin already live there. Anywhere you go on Earth there are all the plants you need to support you, with the exception of the polar caps, of course. Get to know the plants that surround you and let them teach you."

Thank you for talking with me and sharing your wisdom.

Mazra came back and said I should practice with plants at home because there is more to come and practicing will help my understanding of the process.

*   *   *   *   *

For the next two days I could not focus. Too many images kept coming in and interfering. I got to Machu Picchu but couldn't hold my focus there. The third day I was a little better but still there were many images.

Mazra took me to a room where the Dreaming Women were. I'm not sure what they said—something about handling energy. They told me to sit on the terraces leading to the Moon temple. I did and saw a red flower and tried to talk to it. All sorts of strange images from past, present, and future kept coming in.

The flower told me to eat it, which I did.

It then explained: "This area is a vortex and a portal, and it is difficult to stay focused in this much energy. One does it with intention and shielding."

I was a little confused about shielding. It seemed the opposite of being open.

It said, "No, it just doesn't allow all the energy to enter. The intention involves lines of light attaching to the part you want to focus on. Some areas are naturally shielded because of the intention put into them. Like the Moon temple."

It also said something about surrender. I need to look up the word "surrender."

I had been gone too long. The plant said we could continue tomorrow. I said goodbye to Mazra and left.

90

*   *   *   *   *

Feeling much more focused today, I flew off to meet Mazra. She said that I first needed to talk with the flower again.

I went to the terraces near the Moon temple and found the red flower. Everything was so much clearer and in focus. I sat in front of the flower and sent it love.

"It is nice to see that you are channeling the energy better today. Your intention is much stronger. We need to talk more about energy. Awareness of energy is important. Rather than using your physical senses, you must learn to sense energy in a different way."

But how do I know if what I am feeling is real? If I focus on my hands, I feel something, but I think that it may be that I feel it because I am focusing there.

"Of course it is because you are focusing there that you feel the energy. The energy is there all the time, but you are only aware of it when you focus on it. For example, your skin senses your clothes pushing on you all the time, but you do not consciously feel it unless you focus on it. Being aware of the energy in and around you requires focus. Hold your hands out and feel my energy."

I did this and felt a stronger energy near the plant.

"Everything gives off energy and each thing is different in the energy it gives off. Living things have different energy than inanimate objects, and the energy of inanimate objects is different still from spirit energy. When you become aware, you can recognize things by their energy. Stand up, close your eyes, turn around a few times, and then try to find me by feeling my energy."

I did this and could easily feel where the plant was.

"Sometimes it is a feeling in your hands or your belly. Or maybe just a knowing. You need to practice energy awareness so you will become more familiar with what the energy of different things feels like. If you are familiar with my energy and wish to find me somewhere, then you can scan around until you feel the energy which is mine. I can tell when you are coming up the path *by your energy. There are also many more larger networks of energy, but I will let the Dreaming Women tell you about that."*

Thank you for helping me with this understanding. Is there anything I can do for you?

"Send me loving energy and leave me a strand of your hair."

I sent loving energy to the plant and put a piece of my hair by its base.

Mazra was waiting and led me up to where the Dreaming Women were gathered.

"We are happy to see that you are moving forward again. We want to begin speaking about the larger energy systems in Earth. The magnetic lines of energy, or ley lines, direct the flow of energy in the Earth itself. These are similar to meridians of energy which direct the flow of energy in your body. Where several of these lines cross is a vortex, or concentration of energy. This would be similar in some instances to a chakra in your body. Smaller ones might be like pressure points. The energy of a vortex can be used in many ways depending on the intent of the user. It essentially magnifies whatever energy is brought into it.

"Another energy spot is a portal, or doorway. This might be similar to the sensory systems in your body and is used for communication with the rest of the Universe. Portals can be natural or they may be created. The place where you are now sitting in your physical reality is a portal which you created by using it many times to leave and enter your reality, going to and from other dimensions. Entry is easier in a portal than in other places. Some portals are small and some are quite large. The whole area here is a portal which was natural but has been expanded over time with our use. This area is also a vortex.

"One of our concerns is with monitoring the health of Earth in terms of these energy systems. Often people are drawn to vortexes because of the energy there, and in your world, many dangerous and polluting structures have been built on vortexes. This magnifies the negative effects created there. Ley lines have also been broken through mining and taking things out of the Earth as

92

well as through the depletion of water in many critical energy areas.

"The cutting of trees is like taking the lungs away from Earth. You must think of the body of Earth as parallel to your own body. Humans in your time are to Earth much like the bacteria, disease, and cancer that ravage your bodies. To restore health, the energy lines must be respected and maintained.

"The portals must also be better understood. The one in which we live here is used for communication with other parts of the Universe. Sky Beings come here and we learn from them and they from us. But we will talk more about that later.

"We wish you to have with you next time the object which you received when you were in Machu Picchu several years ago. We will show you how to use it."

I got up to leave and Mazra walked out with me. I mounted Cloud Dancer and flew home, feeling much better.

*   *   *   *   *

I went to meet Mazra after checking the energy flow in my body and breathing into it. She took me to the open area where the large rock with the four directions was. You could look out over the mountains from there. I thought it faced West but I was not sure. The Dreaming Women were there. They indicated that this was a very high energy area and I needed to stay focused with intention. I was getting some interference today—things were not quite as clear as yesterday. They asked me to hold the stone in my left hand and try to determine what its use was. The stone fit perfectly into my left hand, and I focused on the energy coming from it. I had the sense that it was a meditation piece and decided to ask it if it was.

It answered, "I was carved by a woman about your age to help her focus in her meditation. She did not see me as a source of energy, only as a channel or focus point for the energy. She made me to represent symbols of the Dreaming Women and the plant women here. The bird beak and wide eyes represent the freedom

93

of flight to other realms and the women's visionary abilities. The other parts represent the seed which is sewn here and a recognition of the male aspect which is necessary to balance the high female energy here."

The Dreaming Women continued, "You need to continue to practice your awareness of energy, and it would be good to work on the meditation piece which was given to you in the Moon temple. Such pieces help to channel the energy and improve your focus.

"There are two kinds of beings from places other than Earth who have come here over many thousands of years. There are the Sky Beings who land their craft on the hill where you land, since that is the center of the portal. They look somewhat like us and we share information about energy systems. There are also the beings who are from another dimension who often appear to us individually as teachers. Tomorrow the Sky Beings will arrive and you will have a chance to meet them."

I headed up to get on my horse and was having a difficult time maintaining my focus.

*   *   *   *   *

Yesterday I made the meditation piece out of catlinite. I didn't quite know how to make it look like what Mazra gave me, but I just kept working on it and it turned out very well.

I met Mazra on the hill and led Cloud Dancer off to the side, because Mazra indicated that the Sky Beings would be coming. The Dreaming Women were standing nearby and we went over to them. We all sat in the sunshine of the beautiful day and one began to speak.

"We need to talk a little about the Sky Beings."

I asked how they knew that the Sky Beings would be coming today.

"It is a knowing, perhaps like telepathy. It is no different from when you know anything before it happens. There are Sky Beings

from many different parts of the Universe, and they all have different purposes for coming to Earth. We are at peace with them all, and they have been coming here for a long time to gain information. We are able to communicate well because of the high vibrational rate we maintain. They appear to us usually in human form, although that is not how they appear or function in the places where they come from. They have mastered the art of inter-dimensional travel or they would not be able to journey here. We'll let them tell you more."

As I looked up, three saucer-like ships came in and hovered and then set down in the field where I usually landed. There are circular marks on the ground there. Several men and women, who appeared human and had light hair and skin, came out. We walked with them into the room where I had met before with the Dreaming Women. I was introduced and we exchanged greetings.

One man addressed the Dreaming Women: "We have news of unrest both in other parts of Earth and in other parts of the Universe."

"We are aware of the unrest on Earth. What is happening elsewhere?"

"There is dissension regarding interference with what is happening on Earth. Some feel that they need to intervene and control the developments here."

A Dreaming Woman responded, "Are they not aware of the universal rule of non-interference? Destiny must play itself out. The presence here of this woman from our future is an indication that things will turn around and humans will more universally understand the role of Earth and its mission."

The man said, "Yes, I can see that it is possible that humans will develop a greater awareness of and appreciation for the energy system."

"Perhaps you could explain to her the purpose of Earth," said the Dreaming Woman.

"As I know you have heard," he said, "Earth is the heart chakra of the Universe and therefore pivotal in how things move and progress in other areas. Just as you have learned that the

Earth is a body which is analogous to your own body, so does the Universe itself exist as a body with an energy system functioning much the same way. In the human, the heart is central to proper functioning and balance. It is the center of the seven chakras and the point where the energy of the lower chakras is propelled into the higher chakras. It is in the center of the paths on which energy flows through the body. The task of humans is to learn to consistently operate from the heart chakra and thus allow Earth to function as the heart chakra of the Universe."

"We will do ceremony to help with the unrest that you report," said the Dreaming Woman.

He responded, "That will be much appreciated. The energy you create is multiplied and expanded into the rest of the Universe by the vortex here. Are you aware of how beautiful this place is from space? Perhaps we should give you a ride sometime."

I see its beauty when I fly in each time, I said.

"That's right," he said. "I forgot that you regularly travel around without your bodies. We will be leaving now but will return soon."

We all walked up to the hill and they went into their ships and soon departed. The ships were very quick and quiet.

Mazra turned to me and said, "You will join us next time as we create a ceremony. Bring your meditation piece."

*   *   *   *   *

I went with my meditation piece to Machu Picchu. When I got there, Mazra led me to a place where the spring flowed over a stone wall and made a little waterfall. It was a very beautiful spot, enclosed by rocks and flowers. She said I should bathe and then rub herbs over my body as preparation for the ceremony. I did that and then we joined the Dreaming Women and a couple of the plant women who were in training to become Dreaming Women.

I asked if all the Dreaming Women had been plant women first. She said they had.

96

"If one cannot intimately understand the smaller levels of energy systems, you certainly cannot work with the larger ones."

I also asked whether she was a Dreaming Woman.

"I was initiated as a Dreaming Woman a few years ago. My job is teaching and that is why I am escorting you on this journey."

We walked with the other women up to the Moon temple, singing as we went. We entered and sat on cushions around the crystal in the center. The Sun had just moved to where it was shining down on the crystal, filling the room with rainbows. The eldest woman, Zasay, led the ceremony.

All the women had meditation pieces and I was surprised to see that theirs were the same as mine. I sensed the meaning of the simple shape. The empty circle is the Moon, the Earth, and the Universe being held in the arms of the Goddess. It also represents the heart chakra of the humans.

Zasay said, "Take the rainbow light into yourselves and use it to heal, clear things away, and raise your vibrational rate. Remember to focus it on those areas which need it."

I focused first on my throat chakra and then on my third eye. When I put the light into my third eye, it felt very healing.

She then asked us to move the energy through our heart chakras. The energy started to move counterclockwise around the circle, forming a visible rainbow of light above us. This light she sent to the people of Earth who needed heart chakra healing.

We formed this ring of light again, moving it through our heart chakras, and sent it to Earth. It sank through us and seemed to be pulled into the center of the Earth. The next circle of light we sent to the Universe. The energy gathered and then went spinning off into the Universe.

At that point, the Sun shifted and the rainbows were no longer there. As I looked around at the women, they all glowed with light energy. Zasay said the mediation pieces would hold this energy for us.

Mazra said I had a little more to learn there, and then we would do a completion ceremony.

When I met Mazra in the field, she said, "Let's go down into the gardens and sit and talk a bit. You are beginning to understand the systems of energy and becoming aware of all that exists beyond the physical. There is much more to learn but our time together is short. The Dreaming Women have asked me to invite you to become a Dreaming Woman."

I'm not sure what all of this means or whether I am knowledgeable enough.

"It means a commitment to understanding, awareness, and support of the energy systems both within you and outside of you. Also a commitment to carrying this tradition back to your time and place and teaching it to others. You will be expected to keep in touch with the Dreaming Women here. You are of course linked to them energetically, and the meditation piece which carries this energy was given to you in the hope that you would make the choice to join us.

"The contact with the Dreaming Women here can be helpful by giving you information on the larger energy systems and things which might affect your time and place. As you learned from our Dreamtime sisters: all that is, exists now. As we see your future, there are always many possibilities, some more probable than others, and we can give you information on probable energy effects."

I think what you are describing is what I am already committed to, so I accept your offer.

"Good. You will need to do much more plant work at home, and your wisdom will grow as you expand your awareness. Tomorrow we will do an initiation ceremony for you and the two other plant women you met yesterday. All you will need is your meditation piece."

I think I'll walk through the gardens before I leave.

"Good idea. I was about to suggest that."

I walked along the terraces looking at the beautiful plants and flowers. A plant with two blue flowers suddenly caught my attention. I was staring at the flowers, thinking the plant perhaps had something to say to me. By looking at the plant in my right visual field, I suddenly saw an image of a man with a white beard and long, white hair. He was wearing some sort of hat.

He said, "You noticed me. I am a teacher in spirit form which Mazra spoke of. It's good that your perception of subtle energy has improved. If you move from your left to right vision, you make the subtle energy perceptible."

Mazra walked up.

"So I see you have met Archimes. Your vision is improving. There is much more you could learn here, but you really need to work with the plants and spirit teachers in your place and time to complete your learning."

I thanked her and headed on up toward my horse.

"Remember the initiation is tomorrow," she called after me.

*   *   *   *   *

When I got to Machu Picchu, I realized that there was one saucer in the landing area. Mazra took me to the waterfall bathing area where the other two plant women were waiting. We bathed and rubbed herbs on our bodies. My hair was rolled on the sides and braided down the back with flowers tucked in. She gave us red-orange colored woven wraps which were sewn on the side and tied over one shoulder.

We walked toward the Moon temple. The Dreaming Women, wearing white garments, joined us. There was a taller woman who I knew belonged to the saucer because she looked similar to those whom I had met before, except that she was older.

The full Moon was rising on our way up to the Moon temple and was the color of the robes we were wearing. We sat around the crystal in the center of the room. It was dark except for the light from some beeswax candles. We seemed to be waiting for something. There was soft chanting along with rattles, drums, and a flute.

I finally understood that we were waiting for the Earth to turn. After some time, the moonlight started to come through the hole in the roof and reflect on the crystal. The crystal seemed to glow with an orange-red light and filled the room with that hue. Zasay began to speak.

"We are here to initiate these three women into the circle of Dreaming Women. We have with us a representative of the Dreaming Women who are not of Earth, initiated many years ago. We ask that the energy of all the women who have ever been initiated into this circle join us now."

I felt the room fill up with presence behind me and around our circle.

"These initiates join the many women who are seeded all over the Earth and in many parts of the Universe as sisters. We have all committed to increasing our own understanding of energy systems, teaching that awareness to others, and creating ceremony to balance and restore the energy lines. Each of you initiates will stand and move counterclockwise around the crystal, following the Moon's path around the Earth. Then as we chant and create music, you will dance the dance of the Dreaming Women. This is a chant you can share with all those wishing to learn about the energy."

I moved around the circle as did the other two women. We then danced as the women played instruments and sang. I could not make out all the words, the tune, or the dance, although I tried for a long time. I think I was trying too hard. What I got was something like this: from the smallest flower to the farthest star, the energy moves through our hearts; I hold the Earth in my arms, her heart is my heart and mine is hers; the flowers and stars are reflections of the love in my heart; the center of me is my heart, the center of the Universe is my heart; I see the web of energy that connects us all. This was all more on a feeling level than actual words.

The moonlight shifted as the Earth turned, and the room was once again dark. Mazra said we would meet back in the tipi tomorrow and I should have the complete dance by then.

I said I wanted to say goodbye to Zasay, but she said, "Don't worry, you will see her again."

100

I went to my horse and flew home, feeling very spacey and sleepy even though I had a good night's rest.

*   *   *   *   *

I went off to the tipi and Mariah said to come in. I was still wearing the orange-red robe and had my hair rolled back and braided with flowers. My meditation piece was in my left hand.

"Welcome to a Dreaming Woman. Do you feel better today?"

Yes.

"You try too hard sometimes. It is better to be receptive and to allow things to come. You must trust that they will. So let us see your dance."

They played their instruments and I began to sing and dance what had come to me:

> I am a Dreaming Woman,
> My center is my Heart.
> I hold the Moon in my arms,
> Her center is my Heart.
> I hold the Earth in my arms,
> Her center is my Heart.
> I hold the Universe in my arms,
> Its center is my Heart.
> The smallest flower and the farthest star
> Are one within my Heart.

When I finished, Mariah asked me to lie down on furs in front of her. She, Mazra, and some other women placed a crystal in my heart chakra. It was pink and round but with many small facets on it. It was about the size of a fist. It was slowly spinning clockwise.

Mariah said, "There is enough room now and you have gained the understanding to begin to use it. Remember that whatever is in your heart will be magnified, so be sure to keep it pure. This crystal will send out to all that is around you whatever you are feeling in your heart. Be aware of what you are sending."

I stood up and thanked them. I gave Mazra a small crystal and she said she would keep it in her medicine pouch.

Mariah said, "Tomorrow we begin with the woman who has remained a mystery to you. We have covered many of the basics and now will begin with some specific skills."

I thanked them all, with hugs for Mazra, Calama, Mariah, Akama, and Che li lan, and nods of gratefulness to the rest.

5

Heart Bundle

When I entered the tipi, Mariah welcomed me and called me over to her.

She took me to the third woman on her left, past Akama and Che li lan, and said, "You were right in your feeling that this next woman is from near where you live. She lived there before the Seneca. These next four women will be teaching you some specific skills. Kanuga is an elder in her village—a clan mother. She has much to teach you."

Kanuga had long, gray hair which hung loose, and she was wearing a buckskin dress with leggings and moccasins. I asked if she wanted to go on my horse and she said that was fine. I also asked why I had not been able to see her clearly. She said it was because my mind was blocking the possibility of staying near home rather than traveling some great distance.

We went out and got on Cloud Dancer and flew back to the Finger Lakes area. My mind again kicked in, trying to figure out which lake we were headed for, but Kanuga said not to worry about that right now. We landed at the North end of a lake which was not one of the larger ones. There were hills on either side of the lake. I could see fields of corn near a village. The village itself was small.

Kanuga explained: "The structures we live in are similar to the long house you are familiar with, but we also have round structures for ceremony and gatherings. We grow corn, harvest other plants, and hunt deer. There are many different animals here—moose, deer, bear, mountain lion, smaller cats, coyote, fox, otter, beaver, and many others. This is an abundant land and life is fairly easy for us. We trade with neighbors in all directions and are a peaceful group as are most of our neighbors. We work with several healing traditions and you are here to learn one of them. The Medicine Lodge in which I am an elder is where we will begin working. My name, Kanuga, means 'healing waters.'

"You will have only a short journey home. Come here to the village next time and we will go to work."

                    *   *   *   *   *

I met Kanuga in her village and she began telling me about what she would be teaching me.

"You are here to learn about our healing ways. The Medicine Society of which I am a part uses herbs but we also use other methods. We are called the Heron Medicine Society because the Heron belongs to the elements of Earth, water, and air. The only missing element is Fire, or Sun, which is masculine. Thus, as you would suspect, we specifically address the healing needs of women and those physical, emotional, and spiritual issues that pertain mainly to women.

"There are stories of how Heron taught women about the healing related to childbirth, moontime, and moonpause. Heron also comes in dreams and visions to continue to teach us. I want you to meet the women of this group."

We walked over to a place where five women were sitting under a tree by the side of a stream. We sat down and Kanuga continued.

104

"Next time, we will be making a journey to the mountains at the South end of the lake. There is a place there which we use for women's ceremony. It is sacred ground. We go there this time of year as well as in the Fall, gathering healing herbs and plants on our way."

Is there anything that I need to bring?

"No. Just be ready to travel. We will be walking with light packs."

*   *   *   *   *

When I arrived, the women were preparing to leave and had baskets on their backs with containers for herbs. They had on double-soled moccasins, leggings, and hide dresses. They carried an extra deer hide for a blanket. I put on my moccasins, leggings, dress, and basket and we were ready to go.

At this point, I began to lose focus, drifting off in many directions. I came back and we began walking, but then I lost it again. We got part way down the lake and sat under a big oak tree to have lunch. I just could not maintain focus well enough to continue. Kanuga worked on my third eye, and it felt as though there were attachments which were slowing the crystal's spin. I could feel it spin more, but I still couldn't stay present there. There were all kinds of things interfering. She said they would wait there for me and we would continue tomorrow.

*   *   *   *   *

I met Kanuga under the oak tree on the East side of the lake. I had done some work with my third eye before but was still not feeling really focused. They were packing things up and she handed me my pack. We traveled down the lake to an open spot high on a hill near the South end. I thought this might be the sacred place, but she said it was just a camping spot. There were herbs nearby which they needed to gather.

I kept losing focus all the way. I was trying to keep the crystal spinning, but it kept getting stuck. Kanuga said to keep working on it energetically and with herbs and to meet them there tomorrow. I called Cloud Dancer and left.

My sinuses were dripping both yesterday and today, and I felt very tired and groggy.

*   *   *   *   *

I did some healing work last night and this morning, and I feel better.

I met Kanuga at the camp. They were again packing things up and handed me my basket.

Kanuga said, "We have gathered many herbs. It is almost the new Moon and this is the best time to gather them."

I told her I thought I was more open and ready to focus today. We headed down the trail to the South end of the lake. There was a swampy area there, and a fairly wide stream ran into the lake. We crossed the river in canoes made of birch bark. Actually, there was one canoe on each side, and when we crossed, we used the other canoe to take the first one back. We then headed up a fairly steep mountain which was quite high. When we got to the top, you could look clear down the lake to where the village was. It seemed to be the highest point that we were on, because you could see in all directions.

The women began setting up camp, and Kanuga asked me to join her on a rock ledge which overlooked the lake.

She said, "This is our sacred ground and where we will be staying for a few days. I told you before that Heron is the totem of this Medicine Lodge, and I now want to tell you a story.

"There was a woman who was very ill. She had been to the medicine people of the village and they could not heal her. She felt that she was going to die, so she left the village while she still had strength and walked to this place. Over the hill to the South is a spring-fed pond, and she lay at the edge of the pond, splashing the

106

cool water on her face as she waited to die. She fell asleep, and when she awoke, there was a Blue Heron standing right next to her, looking down at her. At first she thought she might be dreaming, but she was not.

"The Heron said, 'What are you doing out here all alone sleeping by this pond?'

"She was startled but told Heron the story of her illness and that no cure had been found.

"Heron said, 'The tools for healing lie inside of you,' and with her beak, reached into the woman's heart and pulled out a small medicine bundle filled with herbs.

"'These are herbs which your heart says will heal you, and they have been gathered with love and held in your heart. Make a tea using the spring water here and you will be well. Remember always to look within your heart for the knowledge of healing. You and your sisters may call on me and I will teach you more about healing from the heart.'

"The woman thanked Heron, and the bird flew away. After making and drinking the tea from the herbs in the medicine bundle, she was well again. When she returned to the village, she gathered together some women who were willing to learn and together they formed the Heron Medicine Society.

"If you go over the hill, you will see the pond mentioned in the story. Sit there and see if Heron comes."

I headed over the hill and found the beautiful little pond. There was a Heron standing in the reeds at one end. I sat by the water and she slowly made her way toward me.

Greetings, I said to her.

"Greetings," she replied. "You have come here to learn of healing. Healing oneself or others requires coming from your heart, focusing, and moving the energy. The physical is like this water which you can see and which vibrates slowly. The spiritual, or energy, is like the air which vibrates so quickly you cannot see. I know both well. If you have ever watched me fish, you would understand the intensity of focus which is held by my whole being on the fish which is what I desire. The energy is then directed with

that focus toward the fish to catch it. Healing is similar, requiring intense focus which moves the energy. I will share more with you about this later."

I was thanking Heron when Kanuga came up. She said to come back to this camp tomorrow and we would begin.

*   *   *   *   *

When I met Kanuga at the camp, she said we were all going to a very sacred spot today. Kanuga, the five other women, and I headed toward a spot a little to the South and entered a pine forest. The trees were very tall and the ground covered with needles. The sunlight was falling in streams through the trees. The forest was on a side hill facing South, but as we walked through it, we came upon a flat area. There was a fire circle in the center and a round clearing with lots of pine needles. It looked like a perfect place to dance around a fire. We went over to one area near a large tree and sat in a small circle.

Kanuga began to speak.

"In the story of the Heron I told you yesterday, the teaching was that we each have the tools for healing within us, within our hearts. So whenever we heal ourselves or others, we must come from the place of our heart which is our center, or soul. This lines us up as well with the center of the Earth and all that is around us. For that reason, the first step in healing is moving into that space, lining yourself up with the energy of the Universe. We often do this by singing or chanting and calling in all the energy which surrounds us, that of the trees, animals, plants, water, Sky, and so on. The healing becomes more powerful when you take time to set sacred space and call in the energies. We are going to do that now."

The women began playing a small drum and creating rhythms with rattles while chanting. The chant was in their language, so I wasn't getting all the words, but my understanding of it was a sense of calling to all the energies there. I also sensed the energies arriving and standing on the edge of the circle. There

108

were deer, bear, eagle, heron, and tree spirits. An image of a woman appeared, and I knew she was the woman in the story who is now a guardian spirit of this place. The little people of the forest also gathered around, along with some of the smaller animals. The image I got was that the drum, rattles, and chanting created vibration which set the intention and pulled in the surrounding energy to focus it on healing.

At one point, I saw a mother squirrel with its baby come into the circle and approach Kanuga. The baby squirrel had a broken front leg. Kanuga pulled the bones together and closed the wound. Somehow, the large amount of energy there was focused on the leg, and it was healed. The squirrel and its baby left.

Kanuga began to speak.

"Since we are not here to do specific healing but to learn, I want each of you to focus on bringing some healing knowledge forth. See yourself reaching into your heart and taking out a small medicine bundle. Open it and see what information it has about your personal healing."

I reached in and got the bundle. When I opened it, I saw that it was filled with light. I knew it was the inner light which comes from my heart and that I need to learn to use it for healing myself.

Kanuga found the leaf of a plant in hers. She said she had not seen the plant before but would begin looking for it. She said it was to be made into a tea and used as a tonic to increase energy in older women.

The next woman found a crystal in hers. She said it was one she had been given some time ago and now needed to use for healing.

The woman next to her had a song in hers. She said that when she opened the bundle, the song popped into her head. It was a healing chant, and she might sing it for us after she had a chance to work with it.

The next woman saw a stone which looked like a heart. The heart was beating fast, and her sense was that she needed to exercise more to get her heart in better shape.

Another woman saw a picture of a sunset and felt she needed to do some healing work while the Sun was setting.

The next saw a snakeskin which had just been shed, and it told her that she needed to release some things which were weighing heavily on her heart.

Kanuga said, "We now will chant our gratefulness for the teachings which have been shared with us today and for all those energies who have gathered to participate."

Again, they sang in their language, but I understood the message to be of thankfulness and humbleness.

When we were finished, Kanuga said to meet at the camp tomorrow.

*   *   *   *   *

I met Kanuga at the camp and we headed off in a Southeasterly direction, coming to a ravine where the water was flowing swiftly. We climbed down to where there was a nice waterfall with a pool below.

As we were sitting by the pool watching the water rushing by, Kanuga said, "This water is like the flow of energy through you. If it keeps flowing and is not blocked, you remain healthy. You have learned to see the flow and find blocks, but you need to be more aware of your body as a field of flowing energy. What you see and experience of your body on a physical level is like a mask which covers this energy field. It is the energy which determines health or illness. You need to be more aware of the movement of energy within you. If you do daily ritual to move this energy, you will stay healthy. Of course, you also need to do basic body maintenance—drink pure water, eat nourishing food, and rest. These things are important because they directly impact the energy flow.

"Energy moves through your body as water moves in a stream. A good exercise to help you become more aware is to listen to water moving in a stream and then tune into the more subtle energies moving in your body. Water can also represent the point

110

of stillness within our center where we perfectly reflect all that is around us. But now we are more concerned with its dynamic nature in order to teach you awareness of energy movement."

I had been wanting to stand under the falls since we arrived, and Kanuga said to go ahead. I stood on a rock under the water, letting it pour over the top of my head and down my body. The water was quite cold, but it felt very invigorating. When I came out, Kanuga suggested we climb back up to the top of the ravine to sit in the Sun.

As we sat on warm rocks in the Sun, she said, "There are many methods of healing, but learning to be more aware of the energy movement within your body as prevention is the best method. Once a block has been created, it is more difficult to get the energy to move well again than it would have been to keep it moving in the first place."

I'm not sure how to gain this awareness.

"It takes attention and practice. You will learn. Stop frequently throughout your day as well as in the morning and evening, close your eyes, and see if you can feel the energy movement. If it feels as though it is slowing down anywhere, then focus on moving it. Next time, we will talk about light energy and healing."

* * * * *

I was feeling fairly focused and rested today. I told Kanuga that I had taken the last two days off instead of just one, since yesterday was the first day of my moontime, and I spent the whole day quietly beading and doing other creative work.

She said that was fine.

"We have been doing our own work here. Today I want to talk more about self-healing."

I have a question about our work. It is clear we won't be finished by the time I leave for Montana. Will we continue during the time I am in Montana?

"Yes, there will be times you will journey while you are away, although not as often as now. Everything is on schedule. Don't worry about timing.

"The purpose of your lessons with us is to learn to heal yourself. You have learned the preliminaries and have become more aware of the energies within and around you. It is, as always, a process, and your ability to be aware will improve over time. We now will move to the specifics."

Before you begin, I have another question. I have heard from some that you should never heal yourself because it could lead to ego involvement, but I do not feel that is true.

"It may be true for some who use healing for gaining personal power for selfish reasons. In our traditions as taught by Blue Heron, we must learn to heal ourselves before we can heal others. Through healing ourselves, we learn that the source of the power that heals us is from lining up our hearts with the Heart of all that is—the Creator. There can be no ego involvement when that is understood from experience on a feeling level.

"There are four beams of light which come from your heart chakra when you are centered with this universal energy. You become a vessel through which that energy moves. Those beams of light can then be directed by your will to the area of your body which needs healing or through your hands which can then be held over or on that area. Sometimes it is easier at first to use your hands. The crystal placed in your heart by the Grandmothers will intensify the energy.

"Try that now by seeing the light beams and then let them run down to your hands and then hold your hands over your forehead. Can you feel the energy?"

Yes, but on what should I be focusing?

"There are two aspects which create the healing. One is the intensity of the energy coming through you, and the other is the focus. In most cases, it is not necessary to focus on a specific physical process, but it can be done. Usually it is enough to develop an image for moving the energy, seeing the blocks as darkness, and changing them to light, for instance, or seeing the

energy as a river which is moving. You will find the right image for you. The intensity of energy affects the speed of healing.

"For the most part, your focus is good but you need greater intensity. The amount of feeling present is often an indicator of the intensity of energy coming through you. You must feel as though your heart is the center of the Universe with powerful love energy pouring from it. Practice. Improvement comes with practice.

"Another related aspect of self-healing comes back to energy awareness. When you eat food, use herbs and medicines, you will enhance their effectiveness by being aware of the energy involved. Things work very slowly on a purely physical level. On an energetic level, things move quicker with a higher vibrational rate. Since working on an energy level heals the physical, the energy aspect of the herb or food is more important than the physical aspect. Most of the time you are only aware of the physical aspect of what you put in your body. You must achieve greater awareness on the energy level.

"These lessons are not easy, so we will be taking some time with them. Be patient with yourself, but practice. Tomorrow we will meet again with the other women and talk more about self-healing."

*   *   *   *   *

I felt very sleepy today. The phone woke me up early, and even before I got to the camp I was distracted.

Finally Kanuga said we were going with the other women to the pond. The Blue Heron was at the far end of the pond and slowly moved closer to where we were sitting.

I lost focus again and I told Kanuga I wasn't sure this was going to work, but she said I needed practice in focusing when I was feeling this way, so I tried harder.

The women began talking about self-healing.

The first one said, "I have been having difficulty in feeling worthy of the healing power. These feelings create a block at the heart level, and it is difficult to move the energy because of the block. In order to remove the block, I need to feel worthy. Blue Heron helped me understand that everyone is worthy to be a vessel for the Creator's energy."

The next woman said, "Anger blocked me from healing. So I saw the anger as a dark spot which became smaller and smaller."

I asked whether she needed to deal with the source of her anger, and she said, "Not if I replace it with love and light."

Another woman said, "I did not pay close enough attention to monitoring the flow of energy in my body, and I developed a physical problem. I was blaming myself for not being better in awareness, and I now see how that blame created a block to my healing."

Kanuga said, "It is important to remember that none of us is perfect at this. You will never come to a time where you are totally aware and never have the slightest block. But you will grow stronger in your awareness and you will become wise learning from your blocks.

"Tomorrow we will be doing a ceremony."

*   *   *   *   *

Kanuga said we would be doing the ceremony by the pond to honor Blue Heron's teachings. We sat near the edge of the pond, smudging with cedar smoke and sprinkling water on us and around the circle. This honored the elements of air and water. There was an opening in the circle near the water, and after we all sat down, the Heron came wading through the water and moved into the open space in the circle.

We were honoring the gift Blue Heron gives us: the knowledge that all tools for healing are within each heart. We breathed into our hearts and became aware of the energy within and around us. Breathing in and out from our hearts, we focused on the energy moving within us and then on our connection to the energy around us.

As we were breathing, this message came to me: "Become more aware of energy with each breath."

114

A song and dance were offered by the women to honor Blue Heron, but I couldn't focus enough to get it. Kanuga said it would come into my awareness later.

It seemed as though there were too many things to do today. I am leaving tomorrow for Montana at 5 a.m.

*   *   *   *   *

I finally had a chance to journey again toward the end of the week I was in Montana. Several times a day, however, I had been working on moving the energy in my body.

It seemed different going to meet Kanuga from where I was in Montana. She said she was glad that I was working with self-healing but that I still need more intensity of energy.

I still don't have the song and dance. She said it was because I had not had time to focus on it, and I should try to hear the words first and then the rest will come.

I tried and it seemed like this: "Heron, reach inside my heart and pull out the medicine bundle for my healing. Help me focus the light from my heart, from the heart of the Universe."

I still don't quite have it, but I will have time later today to work on it. Kanuga said to return tomorrow if I had time.

When I was going to bed, I focused in on the song and this is what came:

> Blue Heron, Blue Heron,
> Our sister and our medicine teacher,
> Reach your beak within my heart,
> Help me find the healing ways.
> Blue Heron, Blue Heron,
> Our sister and our medicine teacher,
> Find the light within my heart,
> Healing light within my heart
> Blue Heron, Blue Heron.

*   *   *   *   *

I did not have time again to journey while I was away, so when I got home I flew to meet Kanuga who was waiting and happy to see me.

"Welcome back," she said.

I said it was good to be back with her again.

"You have done well with healing yourself while you have been gone. It is important to keep practicing on yourself. This doesn't mean that you will always be able to instantly heal anything that you want to. We come here each year for a month to learn more about healing ourselves. This is also what you will teach others—how to heal themselves. Each person will use her or his own method. Each person's methods might not work for someone else."

How can I help people tune into their own healing methods?

"In the same way that we do. When you first came here with us, we did a meditation of reaching into the heart to get the heart bundle and then opening it to see what the healing message is. Try that now for healing your left thumb and see what you get."

I closed my eyes and pictured my heart bundle and opened it. I got the sense of using my right hand to send energy and seeing the light from my heart running down my left arm to my thumb. I tried this and when the light from my right hand connected with the light in the thumb, I could feel the energy. I also sensed that I needed to do this frequently.

"You need to make a heart bundle and put in it all that you have learned about self-healing so that when you need it, you can use it as an altar for your heart bundle meditation."

What about the turtle rattle that came to me on my trip?

"We will talk more of its use tomorrow. In the meantime, work on making a heart bundle. You will need it by the end of the week."

116

Kanuga was waiting and I had a sense that what she wanted to teach me was about raising the energy level for healing.

"You have learned the necessary components of healing: being a clear channel for energy, holding your focus, and raising the energy level. I want to tell you more about raising a greater intensity of energy for healing. There are many ways to do this but most involve using a ritual of some kind. We talked before about the importance of ritual, but it is extremely important when doing healing work. Energy can be increased with activities such as singing, chanting, dancing, and prayer, but we often use a combination of rattling and chanting or praying to do this.

"The turtle rattle which came to you is to be used for this purpose. The rattle feels strange to you because of its power. It was made for healing ritual. Turtle is a symbol for our Mother Earth and all her healing energy, and turtle is also a water animal and can call that healing energy as well. So, sit down here and let me show you how we might have her help us."

I sat and Kanuga began to shake the turtle shell rattle around me.

"Whether you rattle in a clockwise or counterclockwise motion will depend on the specific kind of healing, but it should always be circular to build the energy. See if you can feel the energy building as I sing."

She rattled around me and sang:

> I call on the power of the four directions
> I call on the power of the winds
> I call on the power of Mother Earth
> I call on the power of Grandmother Moon.
> Father Spirit, send your healing light
> Sister Turtle calls for your healing light
> Father Spirit, send your healing light
> Sister Turtle calls for your healing light.

After a few minutes, I felt the energy all around me.

"Pull the energy into your heart. Open your heart to make a container for this healing energy."

As I did this, I felt the light streaming from my heart and into my hands which were tingling with the energy. I used the light on my left thumb and on my sinus area.

"Practice this. Work with the turtle rattle and don't forget to make the heart bundle."

*   *   *   *   *

I worked with the song and the turtle rattle before journeying. I felt as though I wasn't quite sure how to use it.

Kanuga explained more about it: "It is best to use the rattle while standing and calling the powers by singing the song. To build energy, you need to be very focused with the intention to call those energies into your heart. The rattle will be even more powerful as you put your own energy into it by creating beadwork on its neck. Remember to set the intention for healing with each bead and use the color red underneath the beads.

"As you learned from our sister Mazra in Machu Picchu, your life must become a ritual of joy and intention as you go about your daily activities. Awareness should be focused on the intention for that activity by creating ritual around it. Everything is sacred and it is important to treat these activities in a sacred manner. Ritual is essential for self-healing because it magnifies the intention and healing energy. You must continue to practice this.

"We are inviting you to join the Heron Medicine Society. Being a member means that you will continue the practice of self-healing and will teach your sisters about the self-healing process while you facilitate their healing."

I would be very honored to be part of this Medicine Society with you.

"Good. We will initiate you tomorrow and that will bring completion to our work. The new Moon is the following day and

we will be headed back to our village, gathering herbs along the way. Don't forget your heart bundle for tomorrow. And work with the turtle rattle before you come."

I won't forget. I will be making the bundle today.

* * * * *

I worked with the rattle and song and developed a ritual dance for using the rattle to call in the energy. When I sat down, I felt the energy buzzing in me.

Kanuga talked to me as she dressed me for the ceremony.

She said, "Two traditional things worn and carried by the members of the Heron Medicine Society are a Heron feather in the hair and a Heron wing fan."

I could see very clearly how they were to be made.

"You are correct in feeling that it is necessary to make a bag for the turtle rattle. It is not to be left out in the open. It would also be a good idea to smudge it before use as part of that ritual.

"It is not that such objects are necessary for healing work. They are only symbols of knowledge you have already attained. In the beginning, they are often teachers about energy and ritual. But after you have used this turtle rattle for a time, you can get the same effect by imagining its vibration and doing the same ritual. It is not the object which is important but the energy it carries, and energy can be present without the object."

She dressed me in buckskins as she spoke.

"You have chosen well for your heart bundle. The purple crystal is awareness of energy flow, and the red meditation stone reminds you of the need to align yourself with the energy of the Universe. The pink crystal turtle symbolizes the raising of the energy through ritual. The red pouch reminds you that all healing must come from the heart and be focused, loving energy. Let's go to the initiation now."

We walked over the hill to a spot near the pond. The other women were already there. As Kanuga began, she called for the

other members of the Medicine Society to be present in spirit form.

She also called in the animal helpers. A turtle crawled out of the pond and waited just outside the circle, while Blue Heron came and stood in our circle as well.

Kanuga spoke to all: "This is a woman who has learned and will continue to learn about self-healing, and she is willing to share that knowledge with her sisters so that they may learn to heal themselves. She understands the importance of creating beauty around the tools used for healing and ritual. She joins us now as a sister in the Heron Medicine Society."

I thanked them all for their teachings and walked over to Blue Heron, stroking her neck and thanking her for the wisdom. She gave me a feather for my hair.

Kanuga said, "Come back and journey with us each year if you wish."

I asked if I could sing the Heron song for them. I did and felt very joyful in doing so. It was sad to leave them but I felt complete. Kanuga said we would be in the tipi tomorrow and told me to bring the heart bundle and Heron feather. I said goodbye to all and left.

*   *   *   *   *

I chanted, using the turtle rattle after smudging it, and then flew off to the tipi. I entered and sat for a moment, looking at each of the women. I could see the last three women more clearly, and when I looked at the old woman next to Kanuga, she changed into a white buffalo and then back to an old woman.

Mariah said to me, "It's good to see you again. It seems as though it has been a long time."

Which is exactly what I had been thinking.

"You are doing well in learning the specific techniques of healing and will continue learning new skills with our sister from Africa next time. You must remember to be intentional in your self-healing, setting aside the time and using ritual. You will become

more effective with practice. Your heart bundle is beautiful. Come up and lay down so we can work with your crystals."

I lay down in front of Mariah, and the women gathered around. They checked the crystal in my third eye and said it was doing well, almost up to normal speed. They also checked the one in my heart and said that it and the stones in my throat were also fine. Then they placed a yellow, orange, and red crystal in my belly.

"This is to intensify the passion—the fire within—which develops in this chakra."

Last, they placed a smoky quartz crystal in my solar plexus.

"This is your balance point and place of personal power which comes through balance. It is also the color of the Blue Heron."

I realized when I visualized this that on my heart bundle I put a beaded trim with a smoky gray bead next to the red leather and an orange-red bead on the outside. These were the exact colors of the crystals they had placed in my power and emotional chakras.

Then Mariah asked me to get up and sing the chant and do the dance that I use with the turtle rattle.

I did so and she said, "You have found the dance which belongs to that rattle. Use it whenever you heal."

6

Rhythms of Healing

I flew to the tipi and entered.

Mariah called me over and said, "It is time to meet our sister from near what is now Kenya. She will teach you about rhythms and emotions."

Mariah took me over to her and I asked her name.

She said, "I have many names, but what I am called in this circle is 'Marumba.' Shall we go to my land?"

I said yes and asked if she wanted to go on Cloud Dancer. She said that would be fine, so we mounted and flew off.

The land in that area was hilly, and we headed for a valley which had a river flowing through it. There was a village beside the river with a large number of grass huts. There were also fields along the river where crops were being grown.

I kept sort of nodding off and finding it difficult to stay focused.

She showed me a hut which I could use during my stay there. She seemed to be a ceremonialist and said she had been busy preparing for the young girls' puberty rites. The weather was warm, and women wore a type of woven, short skirt with no top. Marumba said we would begin working tomorrow.

I flew to meet to Marumba. When I arrived at the village, I had to ask around to find out where she was. Finally I saw her walking toward me.

"Let's go down by the river and talk a little about what you are here to learn."

We walked a short distance to the river and sat on a flat rock near the water which was flowing by peacefully.

"Mariah said you would be learning about rhythms, and that is so. Everything has a rhythm. Your heart is rhythmic, as is the way you walk and move throughout your day. The animals and plants have rhythms, both daily and yearly. Even the trees have a rhythm to which nutrients and water move up and down their trunks. They also move their branches to the rhythm of the wind. The Earth, Moon, and Sun have rhythms, as do all beings in the Universe.

"From your shamanic journey work, you are already aware of the effect different rhythms of the drum have on the body, and your observation that male rhythms are faster than female rhythms is correct. Each emotion also has a rhythm. You could play on a drum the rhythm of sadness or joy. Passion also has its own rhythm.

"Your voice in chanting can create a rhythm which will influence everything around you. Understanding rhythm and its use in healing is the tool we will be working with. I want you to first learn to observe the rhythms in all that is around you. Then experiment a little with producing the rhythms of the different emotions. Next time, we will be with some other women who are members of a women's healing society."

I thanked Marumba for her teaching and started home.

She called, "You are also correct in the meaning of my name. It is 'Dancing Woman' or 'Dancing Mother.'"

*   *   *   *   *

I met Marumba in her village. I was a little distracted just before I saw her when I started thinking about getting a new bridle for my horse. When I saw her, I said I was sorry I was distracted, but I was indulging in an addiction to material possessions.

She said, "Addictions are a disruption to your natural rhythm. Think about that."

I said I would.

She asked if I tried the drumming rhythms for the emotions. I said I did but couldn't differentiate as well as I thought I would.

"You need to feel the emotion and then drum it."

I agreed that I was thinking too much.

"We are going to meet with the other members of the women's healing society today. The meeting will be in the grass hut, since it appears that it might rain soon. Many times we meet outside near the river, and there is a place up river that we go to for ceremony."

I asked if it was near the falls, and she said, "Yes. You have seen it?"

I said I had when I was looking at the area from above.

"We will be making a journey there in a few days. There are five girls ready to be initiated into womanhood, and this is where we will take them. The hut we are going to now is the center for our healing society. In it, we keep various plants which are used for healing, our drums, and other tools for healing. When people come to us for healing, generally it is done there. While mostly women come to us, men also come occasionally for special purposes. There is a men's healing society which they usually go to. Come on in now and meet the other women."

The hut was round and not very large. There were twelve women, including Marumba, all sitting in a circle on woven grass mats. Marumba said that their number varied. The women were various ages and sizes and each had a different hairstyle. They all smiled a greeting.

"Most of the women here are past their childbearing years and have committed their time to doing healing work. We refer to this as a secret society because only members or initiates receive the knowledge of our healing ways. We conduct the puberty rites for girls in secret at the place near the falls. Prior to and during that time, each girl is assigned to one of us as a mentor who will work with her to teach her about womanhood, and as a group, we help her move from the rhythm of childhood to find her own unique rhythm of womanhood.

"We will do some dancing now to give you some examples of what we are talking about. Each of us has our own dance and we also have the dance of our healing society."

Two women went over to pick up drums, and the others stood up and began dancing to the rhythm. As I watched, I saw that each had a different way of moving. Some were fast, some slow, some flowing, and others more abrupt. I sensed that I was to join in and so I stood and tried to allow my body to move with the drums. What I found myself doing was a movement which brought energy up from the Earth to the heart level, at which point I turned and then moved it up to the Sky. The reverse of the movement brought the Sky energy to the Earth.

After this, Marumba asked the women to dance the society's dance. They moved three steps left, hesitated and clapped, moved three steps right, hesitated and clapped, and then put their hands up, waving quickly with a faster foot movement.

After a time, Marumba said to meet her at the hut tomorrow.

*   *   *   *   *

It was raining when I got there, so I went directly to the society's hut, entered, and sat with the other women. Marumba asked if I had worked anymore with emotions and rhythms. I said that I had not because I was working on another healing technique that a teacher had asked me to practice.

She said, "Oh, the triangle. Yes, that is a very good and useful technique. It is not part of the tradition of my culture and so we do not work with it here. *As you are finding, there are many approaches to healing, all valid. When you learn more, they begin to fit together like a puzzle, and it becomes clearer when each technique can be used, by whom, and with whom. The rhythms we use for healing fit very nicely with what you have already learned since they are a way of focusing, raising energy, and healing. Did you enjoy yesterday?"*

Very much. I loved the group dance.

"It has a chant that goes with it as well which we will teach you later today. The dance you did was very much your natural dance. If you recall, the very first time you danced wildly to the drumbeat around the fire in Montana, you did a similar Earth-Sky dance. It is your purpose to be a bridge between Earth and Sky, joining spirit with the physical. The dance will develop more as you continue to learn.

"As you can see, dancing is the main way that we experience rhythms. Dancing the emotion you feel to get in touch with it, and then dancing the emotion you wish to feel is an effective therapeutic method. It is also important to feel the vibrations and rhythms of all that is around you by dancing them. When you dance an animal or tree, you take on its rhythms and become it. This is the first step in shape shifting. When you dance the rhythms of the lion, to some who are perceptive, you will appear as a lion. People who are masters of this technique can appear to others as anything they want if they take on the vibration of that animal or plant.

"We are not, however, concerned here with appearances to others, only with being able to dance the rhythms of all that is around us as a way of truly knowing and experiencing oneness for healing. Now, let's dance and chant a little."

The women began dancing the society's dance in a circle and chanting:

> Rhythm of the Moon, shine in my heart
> Rhythm of the Earth, heal my body
> Rhythm of the Wind, clear my mind
> Rhythm of the Sun, heal my soul.
> Rhythm of the Universe, come into my heart
> Rhythm of the Universe, make my body whole
> Rhythm of the Universe, focus my mind
> Rhythm of the Universe, move my soul.

Marumba said we would be getting ready to start the journey to the falls tomorrow.

* * * * *

When I arrived, everyone was getting ready for the trip. They had woven sacks which held drums, rattles, feathers, and other ceremonial things. A little food was packed, although Marumba said that there was plenty of food available where we were going. I asked how long it would take and she said a day or two, depending on when they got started and how quickly they traveled. She said the mothers were saying goodbye to the girls who were going with us. These girls had started their moontime within the last six months.

I was very tired and losing focus, so Marumba told me to meet them at the falls next time and to practice the rhythms and dancing over the weekend.

*   *   *   *   *

I found where they had set up camp on the South side of the waterfall. It looked as though the path down to the pool under the waterfall was on the other side, and it seemed there might be a crossing up river. They had patched up the roofs of old huts and built some new ones. There was an especially beautiful hut in the center of the camp. It was for the five girls.

Marumba said, "Each girl will spend time alone in it finding her purpose and name. At this point, girls have learned a number of skills, and now is the time for them to find which one they will continue to work with."

Do all women have a trade?

"Yes, men and women share many skills, but some trades are only men's work or only women's work. Both men and women can be drummers and drummakers, but only women cook and prepare food and only men hunt large game."

I asked about the girls' preparation before their first moontime.

"Each girl is assigned a mentor well before her first moontime to learn the physical and spiritual aspects of becoming a woman, so this is really the end point in that learning process. We will start our ceremonies tonight by dancing around a fire. Would you light the fire for us?"

I said I would. The women were coming out in ceremonial dresses, beads, and feathers. Marumba said that most of the time we were there we would be dressed in a ceremonial way. She said I could use some of the ceremonial things in her hut.

At that point, I started to light the fire, and as I did, it flared up and flamed up my front, over my head, and down my back, yet I was not burned.

Marumba, who was watching, said, "That fire has claimed you. It has set an intention for you."

The other women then gathered around and the drumming began. We all danced the society's dance while the five girls watched and then joined into the dance, feeling privileged to be part of this dance. We then went into free dancing, each of us dancing our own dance and the girls trying to find theirs. The older women dropped out, and the girls kept dancing within the circle of women.

Marumba said that we would be doing ceremonies at the pool.

* * * * *

I met Marumba at the camp near the falls. They were ready to begin the walk to the crossing and then to the pool by the waterfall. As we fell into single file moving along the trail which ran through the trees above the river, they began singing a walking song. There were different parts which provided a blend of rhythms, keeping us walking at a good pace.

In about an hour, we reached a place where the river narrowed and a very large tree spanned the river gorge. We crossed and began walking on the trail which led back to the waterfall. We climbed down to the bottom to a nice space beside the pool where the mist gently fell on us. The five girls were taken by their mentors to the edge of the pool, undressed, bathed, and re-dressed in new ceremonial clothing. After they rejoined the circle, Marumba began speaking.

"You now step into this circle as women leaving your childhood behind. You have been taught many things about being a woman, but the most important of these is maintaining the rhythm of harmony. If we feel the rhythms of all that surrounds us today, we know that the water, the trees, the wind, and the flowers all have different rhythms, but they are always in harmony with each other. Listening to them all at once is pleasant music.

"It is humans who have the capability of creating clashing rhythms. The rhythm of anger and sadness create disharmony, particularly if they continue for a long time or occur too frequently. They are also the beginning of disease. As a woman, it is important to always maintain your rhythms synchronous with nature's rhythms. If you experience anger, sadness, or fear, listen for the rhythms of the natural world around you and dance those rhythms so they enter your body and replace those feelings with

130

peace. Of course, one would also look for the source of the feeling in case something needed to be changed.

"I want you young women to enter the circle now and dance the rhythms of the water, trees, flowers, rocks, and wind.... The dance you are doing is beautiful to see even though you each are making different movements in different rhythms.... Now, one of you begin dancing the rhythm of anger.... You can see how out of place that appears and how difficult it is to maintain the rest of the dance with this rhythm present.... If one of you now dances the rhythm of sadness and another the dance of fear, quickly this becomes a very unpleasant experience both for those who watch and those who dance.... Go back now to the dance of the natural world and see how quickly balance is restored.

"You will now begin a period of silence as we move back to our camp and maintain no talking for two days as you turn inward to find your place as a woman within our community."

The women began moving back along the trail toward the camp, singing the walking song. When we arrived, Marumba said that we would do some work together tomorrow while the young women are maintaining silence.

*　*　*　*　*

Marumba was waiting at the camp by the falls.

"The young women are all out in silence. We will meet with the older women at the pretty spot up by the falls."

We walked up and sat in a circle with the other women who were waiting.

Marumba began speaking: "We want to talk to you about the role that you are moving into as Wise Woman. We are giving you a sampling of what our group of Wise Women does. As you can see, part of our responsibility is to educate and initiate girls into womanhood. There are several parts of this process that are essential. The mentorship and teaching of the girl by a Wise Woman is the process by which the girl learns to respect herself and her abilities. The initiation should include a period of silence, *since that is the young woman's first opportunity to seek knowledge as a woman does by looking within. Dancing and rhythm, naming, and other things like that are also good.*

"In your time, this work with young girls is critical. As you complete your initiation into the Wise Woman phase of your life, you must gather other Wise Women into a group and perform this function for your culture.

"We also, of course, do initiations through moonpause into the Wise Woman phase. The same type of process takes place and includes a period of mentorship and teaching, an initiation including a silent period, and then induction into a functioning group of Wise Women.

"You may teach the dance we showed you. While in our community the dance is secret, it is time for many women to dance it in your culture.

"In our village, when a decision concerning the people is to be made, the wisdom women listen to the people and then go inside themselves to find the path which will best serve all the people. No one challenges our answers because we stand as a group in the power of the Earth. There is great responsibility in holding this role, because it is a role of great power which must always come from wisdom and our connection, not from ourselves as individuals. We must always come from a place of restoring harmony of the rhythms, whether in healing or in decision making. Perhaps the other women here can comment on our work."

One woman said, "It is important to remember that this role is one of choice, and not all women who pass through moonpause will choose to become a functioning Wise Woman."

Another pointed out: "It carries great responsibility and time commitment. In order for us to carry out these responsibilities, we must stay in our center and balance the physical and spiritual at all times. Of course, a moonpause woman is fully capable of doing this."

Marumba said, "We want you to see the importance of this work which you are moving into. We will complete our work with the young girls tomorrow when they come out of silence. Then we

132

will travel back to the village where we have some healing work to do which we would like you to participate in. We will do our completion ceremony with you after that."

*   *   *   *   *

The women were all dressed and I quickly changed into a woven wrap. Marumba gave me something to hang around my neck and all of the Wise Women were also wearing them. I'm not sure exactly what it was, but I think it was made from bone.

We went to the spot above the falls. An altar had been prepared for each young woman to sit on, and we stood around them in a circle. Marumba began drumming and chanting, and the others joined in. The words were in their language, but I understood it to be a calling in of the female ancestors.

Marumba explained to me that each of the young women had an opportunity to talk with her mentor after breaking silence. Each of the girls was now asked to stand while her mentor spoke her new woman-name and spoke of her future contributions to the community.

When the first stood, her mentor said, "This woman has been called to teach the children through storytelling. She has a keen memory and has learned many teaching stories and traditional tales of our people. She will begin as an apprentice to our community storyteller."

The second woman stood and her mentor spoke, "This woman is a talented artist and weaver. She already does finger weaving with many different fibers. She will work with our community weaving group."

The third woman's mentor said, "This woman has talked to spirit since she was a little girl and has been called to healing work. She will apprentice with the Wise Women healers."

Of the fourth it was said: "This woman has learned much already about the plants. She knows when to harvest and how to speak to the plants about their uses. They also teach her in her dreams. She will apprentice with the plant women."

133

The last mentor said, "This woman has a way with people. She is very observant and able to tune into what people are thinking and feeling. She wishes to become an arbitrator of differences and will apprentice with the Wise Women arbitrators."

Marumba said, "What gifts you bring to our community! Let us now see your dance."

The drums began and the young women began dancing their own unique dance so that we might truly know them. We all then joined in and danced our own dances. The music became faster and we were all dancing in wild harmony.

When we stopped, Marumba said that they would break camp and head home, arriving late tonight since it was a downhill walk. She said tomorrow we would be doing some healing work.

* * * * *

I went to the society's hut in the village. One of the women was outside and I asked where Marumba was.

She said, "She is in the hut and wants you to come in quietly."

When I entered, I saw Marumba, several other Wise Women, and a younger woman who was pregnant and lying on some mats. Marumba explained that the woman was not due yet but was having some pains and feared for her baby. Some herbs had already been given to the mother to relax her. Marumba asked one of the women to tune into the pregnant woman and dance. Then another woman tuned into the baby and danced. Their movements were followed on drums by two other women. The dance of both was arrhythmic, and the dance of the baby seemed to be a struggle with confinement.

Marumba asked them to normalize the rhythm, while the pregnant women was asked to breath deeply and rhythmically. Marumba placed her hands over the woman's belly and sent loving energy to the baby. The rhythm changed gradually to a steady heartbeat and the dancers followed, becoming peaceful and rhythmic in their movements. Marumba told the woman to practice breathing in this way and to frequently send her baby loving

134

energy with her hands. The woman smiled and thanked Marumba and the other women, and then left.

I asked what had been wrong.

She said, "I believe the baby in its struggling had compressed the cord a few times and was panicking. It also seemed to be a question of the baby having second thoughts about coming into this world. The loving energy helped quiet the baby's fears and the peaceful rhythm calmed the struggle and restored the flow of blood."

At that point, another woman entered limping and sat on the mats. Her lower leg had a gash which appeared to have been there for a few days and was becoming infected. Marumba asked how it happened and the woman was very vague, saying she didn't remember.

Marumba said, "How could you not remember receiving a wound such as this? You do not have to be afraid to tell us what happened."

But the woman still said she did not know.

Marumba put the juice of a plant into the wound and then placed over it a poultice of leaves which had been soaked in hot water. Once wrapped, the woman was helped to her feet and Marumba asked her to dance. The drums accompanied her and she danced with her limp in an odd pattern. The rhythm changed, placing an emphasis on the beat made when her bad leg came down, and her movement began to equalize between the two legs. Marumba asked her to come back tomorrow for more treatment.

When she left, a third woman entered. Marumba explained that this woman had been suffering from a depression since the loss of her child who was killed in a fall. She asked the woman to dance, and again the drums played the slow, arrhythmic accompaniment to her movement. As the woman danced, she began to cry and then raised her fists up in anger toward the Sky as the rhythm became more intense. The drummers gradually changed to a more rhythmic, light beat and the woman's movements changed with it. Soon she was dancing a happy, joyful rhythm and some of the other women joined in forming a circle around her. She began to

135

smile, and when the drums stopped, she received hugs from all present. Marumba told her that she should come back tomorrow to dance again.

Then turning to me, Marumba said, "We have one meeting left here and then we will go back to the tipi."

I hugged her and thanked her for the teaching.

*   *   *   *   *

When I arrived, Marumba took me into the hut that she told me I could use and showed me what to put on. There was a colorful wrap that tied around my waist at the left. It was brown, green, red, orange, and yellow, and it had cowry shells on the edge which came down from the tie. She also gave me a cowry shell necklace and the bone necklace I had seen before. She said to look at it. I took it in my hand and really looked. It was bone carved into an infinity sign.

She said, "This is the symbol of our secret society and we want you to have it. It represents the rhythm of the Universe."

I said I could see that it did and thanked her. She put a flower in my hair and we went to the society's hut.

The women were sitting around in a circle, and in the center was an altar. On the altar was another carved-bone infinity sign, a huge cowry shell, many crystals and gems, flowers, and water from the river.

Marumba said, "Even though you have not yet completed your initiation into the Wise Woman time, we accept you into our healing society. This is why we have shared our symbol, altar, dance, and chant with you. We recognize you as a healer and hope that what you have learned in your time with us will be useful to you."

I said that while I certainly had not integrated it all, I understood the importance of rhythm in all kinds of healing and would be incorporating it into my work.

"You may always return here to learn more from us. Let us see your dance now. It is important for you to keep dancing."

136

137

I got up and began dancing while the drum accompanied me. I began to have a hard time staying focused. They danced with me after a time and then I left.

* * * * *

I went to the tipi, and as I looked at the reverse swastika on the front, I saw it as stationary, but the tipi was spinning to the left, sort of as though the swastika were fixed and the Earth was spinning. Then Mariah said to come in. I entered and sat by the door, looking at the women, most of whom were very familiar to me now. Mariah called me over to her.

"The last two crystals we will place in your body are at your base and crown chakras. They connect you more intensely with Earth and with spirit."

Into my base chakra she placed a very rich, brown crystal. I could feel its connection with Earth and the soil. At my crown chakra was a clear crystal with a fairly long point. It was casting a beautiful white light all around me as well as above me. It looked like a miniature lightning rod which was glowing from the power of lightning. She checked the other crystals and all seemed to be working well.

Then she asked me to dance my dance. The drums began in a soft African rhythm and I began my dance of honoring Earth and Sky.

After a time she said, "Dance as if you were the bridge between Earth and Sky, and the energy moves from one to the other through the crystals in your chakras."

This changed my perception immediately, and I could feel the energy flowing through me as I danced. Then they all joined me in the healing rhythm dance of the secret society.

Mariah said that tomorrow I would meet and begin learning from their oldest member.

7

Good Relationship

I was dizzy this morning when I got out of bed. My body seemed to want to turn to the left as I walked. I muscle-tested to see if I should spin, and my body said yes. Spinning seemed to help.

I entered the tipi and sat by the door, feeling the warmth of the energy there. I looked to my right, and the old woman looked back at me.

Mariah said, "Our eldest will tell you how you may address her."

The old woman said, "We have met before."

It was she who gave me the crystal tooth in the soul retrieval.

"You began working with that crystal and need to continue. You may call me Grandmother for now."

I asked if she wanted to ride on Cloud Dancer and she said, "I'd love to."

When we went outside, I was surprised at how quickly she sprang up onto the horse. With her behind me, we flew off to the West which appeared to be somewhere in the Western part of South Dakota. As we circled, she pointed out one lone tipi in the cottonwoods by a crystal-clear river. We landed and I asked if she lived there all by herself. She said she did but she had lots of people she visited and who visited her. It was a warm day and we sat under the cottonwoods by the river. She began to tell me about herself.

"I have come to many people to teach about the relationship with all things. I have in the past appeared as a young and beautiful woman, but to you I come as a Grandmother, because in your world it is the grandmothers who will bring the people back to good relationship with all things.

"As you began to learn from the crystal tooth, being in good relationship means being one with all things. There is much power in all things around you with which you will learn to work. For instance, at your home, rain is needed. You have the ability to work with the Thunder Beings to bring the rain. The dizziness you are experiencing is from a great influx of energy from the lightning last night which was received by the crystal at your crown chakra."

I said that I never knew when it was alright to call in the rains. I do not want to disrupt the balance of nature.

"You will know from talking with the Thunder Beings what is possible. Nature has already been disrupted. Calling the rains in good relationship can be a restoration of that balance.

"You will need to find a time between now and tomorrow to work with the crystal tooth and also to review what you have already learned from it. We will go on from there tomorrow. You have learned to be aware of the energies around you, and now you will learn more specific ways of working with those energies. The pipe has been a traditional way for my people to communicate with energy, so we will work with that also."

*   *   *   *   *

When I first worked with the crystal, the lesson was about how one might call the Thunder Beings. Basically, the teaching was that to call for help from anything in nature, one needs to become one with it and develop a relationship with it. If I talk to the Thunder Beings and become friends with them, they will come when I call if it is possible for them to do so. When I worked with the crystal again, the message was similar—developing a relationship with everything around me will change my perspective in each moment. I had a sense of the tree which created the wood to make the house I was sitting in. It gave me a reverence and great respect for all that was around me, even in my house.

Grandmother was waiting outside her tipi and we went to sit under the cottonwoods. I was sort of drifting off, and she asked me to be more present there and said she would wait until I could be. I disciplined my mind and tried to let everything else fade away except the tipi, cottonwoods, and river. Then she began to speak.

"We talked last time about a shift in perception where you would be aware of relationship with all that is around you in each moment."

I said that I have glimpses of that but cannot hold it.

"By the time we are done, it will be as natural as breathing. Visible breath means releasing with each out-breath a prayer of gratefulness to all that is around you supporting you—a prayer of love and friendship with all that is there. You spend too much time thinking. Once you have decided to do something, you don't need to think about it anymore. Thinking blocks your awareness. Spend more time in awareness and less in thinking. When you are moving in awareness of connection, there is beauty created around you wherever you go. Thus, to walk in beauty is to walk in awareness of connection. When you do this, your life will then be created in beauty.

"There is a thundercloud over on the horizon. I'd like you to sit here and talk with it. You do not need to call it in unless you want to."

I sat and focused on the Thunder Being. I saw myself in the thundercloud and felt the rain and wind. The lightning was moving past me, and the thunder was clapping. I spoke and said how much I have always loved the visits of Thunder Beings. I love the rain and beautiful light energy coming from the Sky to energize the Earth. The Thunder Being replied that sometimes people feel that the thunder is anger. I said I always loved hearing the thunder. It sounds like giant drums which vibrate all beings in its presence.

Grandmother called me back and said, "Practice with your awareness. Tomorrow we will begin talking about the pipe."

*   *   *   *   *

I did some healing and manifestation work and then journeyed to Grandmother's tipi. I was having a hard time focusing and I struggled to be fully present there.

She said, "You seem to be resistant to this process when you don't know what is going to happen next. You need to trust that what I teach is right for you."

It's not that I don't trust you. It's just that part of me still fears change and doesn't want to see things from a new perspective.

"Change is inevitable, and resisting only slows your soul's journey. How have you done with awareness?"

I practiced yesterday and found that there are many levels of awareness. There is sensory awareness—tuning into my physical senses at the moment. There is energy awareness—energy within and around me. There is also awareness of my thinking and feeling. But I think that what you spoke of—awareness of relationship to things—is still eluding me. I have had moments of awareness of connection to what is around me, but I feel as though I'm still not getting it.

"If you already had it, you wouldn't need to be here learning it. Part of the problem is that you are still feeling yourself as separate. You understand the concept of oneness on a thinking level, but you do not yet hold the feeling. Another aspect of this has to do with exchange which occurs in relationship. You willingly take from all that is around you, but most of the time you don't give back. There needs to be an exchange in relationship. It is good that you sang to the Cloud Beings and thanked them for the rain they brought last night after you requested it. Sometimes

142

just speaking your gratefulness is enough, while other times more is needed. But always there should be an awareness of the gifts you are receiving in each moment and a continuance of the gifting cycle.

"I mentioned yesterday that we would be working with the pipe. You have a pipe now which you do not feel comfortable or connected with. As you suspected, during our time together you will be making a pipe. This process will help you understand its true meaning and how it represents the process of good relationship. The pipe you make will be used for teaching good relationship to others."

I have a question about the shape of the pipe, since I have heard that there are different shapes for men's and women's pipes.

"The shape of the pipe does not matter except that its shape has meaning for you. Continue to practice awareness and remember to give back. Tomorrow?"

Yes, tomorrow.

*   *   *   *   *

I went to Grandmother's tipi after doing some healing work. It was hard to stay focused today because my regular routines had been disrupted due to company.

Grandmother said, "I want to talk to you about the pipe. Making the pipe will be an exercise in good relationship. The stone will tell you how it is to be carved, and the stem should be selected from sumac near your house. Just as the feelings you have had over the last two days are rememberings of oneness and good relationship, the pipe will also be a remembering. Its function in a pipe ceremony is to help people remember through the symbols used.

"In many ways, the pipe is like the turtle rattle. Once you have successfully used it for a time, you no longer need the object. You know the feeling it has helped you remember, and you can access that feeling without the rattle or pipe. Such objects are teachers for those who are learning about energy and oneness. Your soul

already knows these things and is trying to bring them into your conscious awareness.

"You need to begin working on the pipe now. This will be a working pipe, so keep that in mind as you work and make every movement a prayer. Come with me now into my tipi."

I went inside with her. There were furs and buffalo robes and an altar.

She said, "Another thing we will work on is your medicine bag. We will be talking about what needs to be in it, the use of the objects, and how it should be set up."

I was losing focus again, so we agreed to meet tomorrow.

*   *   *   *   *

I did some healing work and then went to Grandmother's tipi. She invited me in again. I looked around. Everything was so neat and beautiful!

She said, "Everything here has meaning to me and was created in beauty. What else do you sense about this space?"

I looked around a bit and then realized that what I sensed was a feeling. The energy here felt wonderful!

"The energy here is also beautiful because I am in good relationship with all that is here. The ground we sit on has agreed to allow this tipi and me to be here for an indefinite amount of time. The poles are trees which agreed to be part of this structure, as did the buffalo whose hides make the cover. The rocks which line my fire pit were grateful to be of service to me, and I am grateful to them for their beauty and use. Even the willow branches which form the backrest you are sitting on are recognized. When you are in good relationship with all around you, great care is taken to use the space well and keep it beautiful. You need to be more aware of this in your home space.

"I want to talk to you about your medicine bag. Many people speak of a medicine bag containing power objects. Objects are powerful when they help you remember. They may do this because of memories triggered from this life or others, but they trigger the

144

remembering of feeling. Only those things which create memories of important lessons are kept in a medicine bag. I would like you to go through your bag and see what is there and reflect on the lessons which are remembered. We will talk more about this and the uses of power objects in ceremony tomorrow."

*   *   *   *   *

We went into Grandmother's tipi again and sat on the willow backrests. She began speaking.

"As you could easily see in looking through the medicine bag, only some things clearly belong there. Your lessons are not yet complete and so there will be more things to come. In the bag are the symbols of your knowledge. Many of the items you have made and acquired during your journeys with us belong there because they are the symbols of your power and wisdom. Otter represents the feminine, playfulness, and curiosity, all of which have led you along your spiritual path. The beadwork of butterflies and flowers represents transformation and beauty, two things which guide your life.

"This otter chose you to become part of this process. When she was trapped, she left babies behind which died. In her belly, she now carries the symbols of knowledge and change which will lead to honoring the animals and protecting the children. Care for her well, as her spirit carries great intention for bringing the feminine into your world.

"How you finish the inside does not matter as long as it is beautiful and orderly. At this time, the bag is to be used on a personal level, not in your work with others. There will be a time when you use it more openly, but not now. It represents your power and wisdom and is to be used in your personal ceremony. Some of the objects in the bag will be used in working with others, and there will come a time when they may be part of a teaching altar. Now is a time of gaining wisdom and building power. You must be very familiar with the use of each object in your personal ritual before you use them with others.

"Tomorrow we will talk more about the pipe, so begin tuning into that energy."

*   *   *   *   *

Grandmother was waiting outside the tipi and she had a bundle on her back.

She said, "We are going to walk down to a pretty spot by the river."

We sat in the grass on the river bank and she began to speak.

"This is my pipe bundle. As you can see, I have made the container as beautiful as the pipe.

"The shape of your pipe will not be traditional. While traditional Indian people are holding energy, which is very important, your purpose is to bring new energy, new levels of understanding to your people. You need to dream the form for your pipe.

"The ceremony with the pipe has the purpose of acknowledging relationship with all that is around us—all that is. It is not so important what words are used, but rather that the feeling of good relationship with all things is created. This includes being in good relationship with everything from eagles and mountains to ants and plastic. In your world, humans feel that some things are not natural because they were created by humans and not nature. All things on Earth are created from the natural elements and as such deserve our respect and good relationship.

"Once the feeling of good relationship with all things has been established, then one might ask them for support in attaining what one needs, whether it be healing, the answer to a question, peace, or rain from the Thunder Beings. The pipe is a symbol which reminds us of our relationship with all that is around us as well as within us. It calls the creative spirit to work through us as we enter the state of oneness with all things.

"The most important part of this is the feeling. Actions may be performed in ceremony, but when there is no feeling, there is no effect of the ceremony. Where correct feeling is present, many

146

different actions can bring the effect. I want you to think of these things as you begin your pipe."

I'm not really sure how to begin.

"You are being guided. Work from your intuition and feeling, not your reason."

Are you White Buffalo Woman?

"Yes, I am that energy. I come to you as a Grandmother to share with you the wisdom which must be carried to your world. There are many White Buffalo Women in your time who will carry this wisdom forward as elders, and you are one of them. We will talk more about the pipe tomorrow."

* * * * *

We went again to the pretty spot by the river to sit, and Grandmother spoke.

"I want to talk more about the ceremony around the pipe. Often there are rules used in a ceremony which say that things must be done a certain way. The purpose of these rules is to create the appropriate feeling for those who do not already have that feeling. The idea is that by following the rule, one would be more likely to have the correct feeling, particularly if the rule is explained. One has a greater understanding of and respect for the symbols of the pipe, for instance, if one knows that the bowl of the pipe is always held in the left hand because the bowl and left hand are feminine. Or, we take off our shoes when holding a pipe, since removing our shoes has long been understood as respect for sacred space—and a pipe is sacred. The rules are not important in and of themselves, but only for the feeling which they create.

"Whatever rules you decide to use with your pipe will develop as you work with it. The pipe will teach you much about its use. You have already used the pipe you now have in creative ways that fit the people and the situation. You need to carry through more on the energy created, rather than letting it drop. It is all part of your learning.

"A song to go with the pipe ceremony, which, again, creates feeling, is also important. You will have a song before our work is done here. Have you dreamed your pipe?"

Yes, I have part of it but I can't quite get the whole thing.

"You must be able to see each part completely before you begin. It will come."

I still feel as though I don't really know how to do this.

"Trust the process and the creative spirit working through you. Work on it today, and tomorrow we will make a journey to a sacred place near here where you will gain more knowledge of this process."

*   *   *   *   *

Grandmother was waiting by her tipi. She closed it up and was looking at the Sky to the Northwest which was quite black.

She said, "A storm is coming but I think it will pass North of us. Will your horse pull a travois?"

I think so.

To make the travois, she attached the poles over Cloud Dancer's withers and lashed two shorter poles across the back end of the long poles. On the travois, she placed a tipi cover, some extra hides, and another bundle. She had her pipe bag on her back and medicine bag at her left side. We climbed on Cloud Dancer and started across the prairie to the Southwest. For an old woman, she moved with great flexibility and grace in all that she did. I asked if we were going to Bear Butte.

"Yes. Many people have seen that as a sacred spot."

I said that I understood, after visiting it this summer, why it is called Bear Butte.[1]

---

[1] When I went to Montana last month, I knew I needed to stop at Bear Butte, although I wasn't sure why. When I walked around there, I understood why I was there—I needed to become familiar with the vibration of the place so that I could return during the journey work.

"Yes," she said. "The great sleeping Bear. The Bear is both a medicine teacher and a dreamer, so we go to sit on the back of the Bear to listen for her dreams and medicine stories."

The country we were traveling through was a very beautiful prairie with hills covered with pines. We followed the river for a while and then cut through a pass in the tree-covered hills and out onto the prairie again. Soon we could see the sleeping Bear in the distance. When we arrived at the base of the Bear, we stopped beside some tipi poles and began unloading. The tipi cover went on quickly and camp was set.

"Tomorrow we will do a purification lodge before we go up on the Bear's back."

I left her there to create more beauty as she set her altar in the tipi.

* * * * *

Felt sick this morning—headache, sinus drip, and upset stomach. It was either something I ate or something I inhaled sitting in exhaust fumes while waiting in traffic to leave a parking lot after a concert last night. I worked on some healing and then flew off to see Grandmother.

She was waiting with the rocks heated and the lodge built and covered. She said we would do four rounds, the first to purify the body, the second to purify the mind, the third to purify the emotions, and the fourth to purify the spirit. I went in with her and even in the complete darkness could see the glow around her.

I asked that all negativity leave my body and that my body be cleansed of all impurities. After stating this several times, I felt a large shift, and my head felt better and the rest of my body felt good. She brought in more rocks and I stayed in the lodge. In the next round, I asked that all limited thinking leave me now and that

I be open to the possibilities. In the third round, I asked that all negative emotion leave me and I began to feel more joyful. In the last round, I asked to let go of any blocks on a spiritual level. When we finished, I felt much better.

She said, "Try to maintain this feeling state. We will wait until tomorrow to go up onto the dreaming Bear's back."

* * * * *

I met Grandmother at Bear Butte. She asked whether I was able to hold the cleansing from the lodge, and I said I thought that I had held it pretty well.

"I want to talk a little about the purification lodge."

I said that what we did was so simple but nevertheless very effective.

"The process is very simple and not too much different from any other healing technique. After setting sacred space, it is a matter of using energy and focus. The energy in this case is created by the heat, and the focus by your intention. Anything else which is done as part of this ritual is to help create the focus either for those who are participating or for the person leading the process. Let's go up onto the back of the Bear now and listen for a song that you will sing to your pipe."

We walked up a path which went toward the neck of the Bear and sat on a ledge which looked out over the prairie and rolling, pine-covered hills in the distance. Grandmother sat beside me and told me to listen to the Bear dreaming. I had a hard time focusing because many images were going through my mind.

She said to hold my focus on the pipe. When I did, I understood that the pipe would sing me its song.

Then there seemed to be some words that could be a song: "Wind, blow through my soul. Carry these prayers on the smoke into Spirit, that my intentions made in good relationship with all things be manifest. Bowl and stem, join for balance and harmony of all things in the circle of life."

But it didn't really sound like a song.
Grandmother said we would come back here tomorrow.

*   *   *   *   *

I felt so sleepy and groggy today. Very tired.

I went to meet Grandmother and she had a purification lodge prepared. I told her that I felt really blocked again and she said the lodge would help.

She already had rocks in the pit when we entered, and beginning with body purification, she said, "May all physical blocks leave now."

Then she sang a chant.

We moved to the mind and she said, "Let the mind be purified and cleansed of all limited and doubting thoughts."

Then the emotions: "I call on the steam from the rocks to carry the heat and vibration of the Sun and Earth through this woman. Surrender your feelings of depression, fear, and sadness to the Earth and step into the feelings of joyfulness. Step into a joyful rhythm in each moment."

Then spiritual cleansing: "Move from a limited being to who you really are—a magnificent, limitless being of light energy. Let go of the old way of being and step into the new way of being."

As she said this, I began to feel better.

We came out of the lodge and she poured water over me and I over her. We dried off, dressed in buckskins, and began the walk up to the Bear's back.

When we reached the ledge, she asked me to sit there by myself a while and be open to what comes. It seemed as if the Bear were speaking to me.

"Moving into good relationship is a process requiring conscious awareness. As you walk forth with the pipe, you walk with a symbol of that awareness, bringing people together in a shared experience of and commitment to being in good

relationship. Your daily activities should not be approached as 'things to do,' but as joyful opportunities to create beauty and good relationship with all that is around you. There is no task which cannot be done in a joyful way, consciously giving good energy to all that is there. Do not be concerned about the right words or ritual in working with the pipe. The pipe knows its purpose. Your task is to come to it with good energy and intent. Step into this new way of being in each moment."

Grandmother came up and said we would talk more tomorrow.

* * * * *

I met Grandmother and thanked her for the healing work she did with me yesterday. I told her that I found more joy in all I did yesterday, and I know how important that is. Everything went more smoothly.

"All of what we have been talking about fits together. Being in good relationship with all that is around you requires awareness, but it also requires you to honor that relationship with positive energy. Love and joyfulness are those emotions which must be cultivated like flowers as you interact with all that is around you. When you feel this way about these things, you naturally want to create beauty in all that you do as a way of honoring everything. There is nothing that you do or interact with that does not deserve your joyful attitude and love.

"When you work with the pipe, it is a symbol of this kind of relationship. It is not a ritual which is done and left behind, but a living ritual that is a gratefulness for all those relations which make our every moment possible. It is a celebration of a new way of being in the world. As I have said before, you will walk into a new time carrying the pipe. The new way of being is being in good relationship with joy and beauty, and the pipe is both the symbol of this and a way of celebrating this. In your time, the pipe is also a way of awakening and calling others to be in good relationship."

I see, Grandmother, how this all comes together. I am feeling it more in my daily life, but it seems difficult to bring it into each moment.

"Not as difficult as it might seem, for this is our natural way of being. It is like coming home to who you really are."

Grandmother, I need to tell you how good it feels to be in your presence. It feels like being home.

"I will be there with you each time you light the pipe and in each purification lodge you do. I also am there as you move in joy and beauty through your day. I am always there wherever good relationship exists.

"I want you to spend some time with your pipe today to listen for its song. If you don't have it by tomorrow morning, bring the pipe with you when you journey and meet me back at my tipi by the river."

Do you need help moving things back?

"No. I have helpers here I will travel with."

*   *   *   *   *

I journeyed to Grandmother's tipi with the roughed-out pipe bowl in my hand. I told her I had not had time to sit with it because I had been busy creating beauty and arranging things so that I had the space to finish working on the pipe.

She said, "Many tasks become quicker and easier when you approach them from a joyful place."

I said that I had noticed that and asked if she had a good trip back.

"It was not a long trip but very beautiful. I see you have the bowl with you. The song comes from within the stone. I want you to go sit with it by the river and move your consciousness into the stone to hear its song. You might also hear its name. Come back here when you have found the song."

I walked down to the pretty spot by the river and sat holding the bowl in my left hand, covering it with my right hand. I let my consciousness move into the stone, to experience its red color and its vibration. I listened but did not hear anything.

Finally I said to the stone around me, may I talk to you?

It said, "Yes, certainly you may."

I have come to find your song.

"I know. White Buffalo Woman sent you to me. Be still and listen and I will sing it for you."

I sat a little bit and told my mind to stop blocking and then I heard the song:

I honor my relationship with all that is
From the smallest ant and flower to the Moon and stars.
I walk in good relationship with all that is
Creating joy and beauty with the way I live.

I sang it a few times and then I heard the word "Starflower."

I said, "Starflower"? Is that your name?

"Yes, because I will help you link the Earth and Sky, the flowers with the stars."

That is a beautiful name! Thank you for sharing your song with me.

I went back to where Grandmother was waiting and sang her the song.

When I told her the name of the pipe, she said, "That is a good name for the work that you are and will be doing. Come into the tipi now."

We walked in and sat by her altar.

"Your work with me is complete for now. I will always be available to you as will my healing lodge. And remember that each time you remain joyfully in the moment, creating beauty with your walk, I will be there with you. I have been called many names: White Buffalo Woman, Star Woman, Rainbow Woman. You may call me whatever you wish, but I will always be present to call you and all those you work with into good relationship."

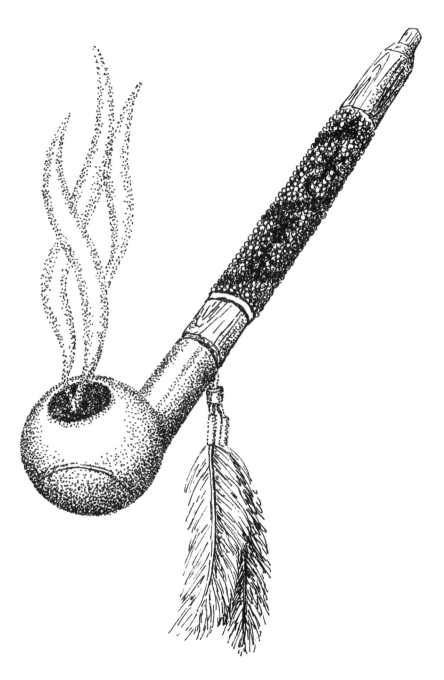

By now the tears were rolling down my cheeks, both in the joy of her presence and the thought of ending this part of our work together.

I said "Grandmother" feels like a good name to call you.

"Tomorrow you will meet us back in the upper world tipi."

I thanked her and started to leave.

She called after me, "Don't forget to finish your pipe and medicine bag soon."

I smiled and said I won't forget.

*   *   *   *   *

I went to the tipi and asked to enter. As I pulled back the flap, it seemed very dark inside. Luminous things were in the air.

Mariah said, "Come in. We were just experimenting with the darkness. Can you tell where we all are sitting?"

I could. They were all in their normal places, and it felt good to know them. There was only one I had not met yet.

Mariah called me to come over and asked whether I enjoyed my time with Grandmother. I said that Grandmother moved me to another whole level of being with her grace and beauty.

"She is an inspiration for all of us as well," she said. "Sing us the pipe song."

I sang, and when I was finished, she said, "That certainly is the essence of what Grandmother teaches."

Grandmother then came over and assisted her, and while I was standing, they checked the crystals in my chakras—rich brown, red-orange, smoky quartz, pink quartz, multicolored stones, clear quartz, and a quartz point on top showering me with white light.

She said, "All seems to be working well. It would be good for you to get a massage to integrate this change more fully into your whole body. As always, eating, exercise, and sleep are important. We are nearing the end of our journey. There are two more of us and then you will write from your own wisdom. We would like you to take the next two days off and concentrate on your pipe and the other things you need to make."

156

8

Community

I arrived at the tipi and entered. There was soft light inside.

I said hello to all, and Mariah called me over to the last woman in the South.

She said, "This woman is from an island South of India which has become known as Sri Lanka. The culture you will visit existed there long ago."

I said hello to her and tried to see more clearly what she looked like. She was dressed in silk and sandals. Her complexion was dark and her hair mixed with black and gray.

I asked if she would like to go on my horse.

She said she thought she could manage that, and so we got on and flew toward her land.

From the air, there was a very large island, and it seemed as if there were large villages in the four directions as well as in the center. We were headed for the village on the Eastern shore. We landed and she began to tell me about her land.

"We live simply in huts and build more elaborate structures of stone for ceremony. While we are isolated as an island, we build ships which carry us to other lands for trading. One of the things you will learn about here is community functioning."

I asked her name and she said, "I am called 'Tinacu.'"

I kept seeing lots of different kinds of objects, dress, and art.

"When we trade with others, we bring back ideas which are then put with our own ideas to create new things, so there is great diversity among my people. Strong community, but great individual creativity."

I asked whether some people were placed above others.

"No. Each person has special gifts which are honored within the community. Tomorrow when you come, we will meet with a group of women and talk more about this."

* * * * *

I went to meet Tinacu in the East village of the large island. She said we would join some women down by the ocean as they welcomed the light of the new day. We walked that way and the sunlight was filtering through a light fog and creating a golden mist.

"Honoring the light is part of the responsibility of the East people. The light symbolizes creative ideas and the light which pulls things from the void to make them real. It also symbolizes the gift of seeing. The people who live in this village are the seers. They spend time visioning and seeing for the rest of the community. It is not that everyone does not have that ability, but it is the East people who have the special gift which they give and teach to others.

"Each of the villages is responsible for a special function. The South village is responsible for building and construction in the physical world. The West village is responsible for dreaming and darkness as well as emotional knowledge. The people of the North village are the accumulators of wisdom and the ceremonial specialists. They also deal with matters of life and death and healing. The Center village is composed of representatives of the four villages, and these individuals create the harmony and decision making."

158

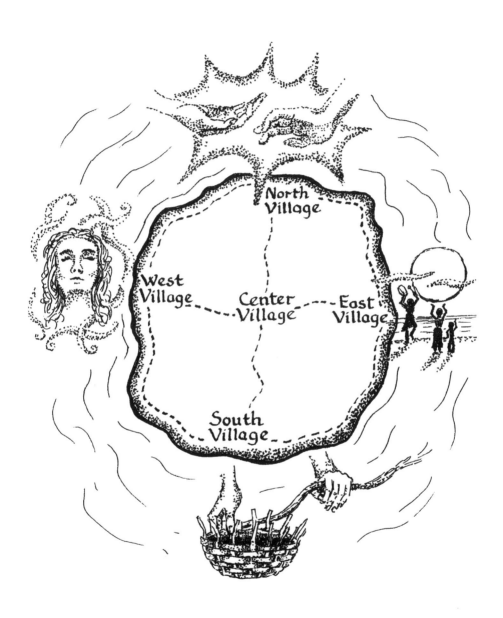

But what about diversity? When you have all the people with a certain gift living together, doesn't that eliminate diversity?

"It is not so much that all people with a similar gift live all the time in the same village as it is that each village is responsible to the whole for maintaining that gift. There are two things which create excitement for positive growth. One is being with others who share your gifts, and the other is being with those who are very different from yourself. Here, when you want to be stimulated in either way, you know where you can find those people. Each village actually has many diverse people who are there to learn about the gifts for which that village is responsible. Now that you have a sense of what the structure is, let's go and join these women."

Are you from the East village?

"No, I am from the Center village but will guide you to each of the villages."

And the women we are joining?

"They are of the East village and will tell you more about their responsibilities. When you come back tomorrow, you will talk to them more in depth."

*   *   *   *   *

When I met Tinacu it was sunrise, and she suggested we go down to the shore to meet the women doing the sunrise ceremony. There were seven women of various ages chanting as the orange ball slowly rose above the surface of the water and hung in the misty Sky. The chant was in their language, but the meaning seemed to be that the Sun was being honored and asked to shine its light on humans to help bring forth their creative light and to help things grow on the Earth. A general gratefulness seemed to be expressed for all that the Sun brings to our daily lives. There were drums and other instruments being played as well, and I noticed that all who lived in the village, wherever they were, turned to face the rising Sun while the chanting was going on.

160

When the women finished, we went to one of the huts which was quite large. Most of the huts were large with wooden floors. Inside this hut, there was a fire pit in the center and benches along the back wall. Mats were arranged on the floor for sitting closer to the center. We sat in a circle on the benches and mats.

Tinacu said, "Heron has come to learn about your lives in East village."

At Tinacu's request, they began to tell me about their work.

The first one said, "As you just saw, one of our responsibilities is the sunrise ceremony. There are different groups of us, both men and women, who take turns greeting the Sun each day. We each have other things we do as well which are related to our own gifts. Some of us are visionaries, some teachers, some craftspeople and artists. So, part of the time each day is devoted to those endeavors. We eat at least one meal each day in mixed groups so our discussions can stimulate each other. We also all have daily living tasks—gathering food, raising crops, cooking, cleaning, repairs—which are equally shared by all. The purpose of our being together is to enhance our own growth process while we give the gifts and knowledge we already possess."

I asked if there was a sense of competition with each other.

"No, this is a cooperative community. Each person's gifts stimulate another's growth and creativity. We recognize that we are all in a process of developing our gifts and becoming balanced within ourselves. Our individual responsibility is to give our gift to the best of our ability at any point in time. We are not expected to be perfect. Equally important as giving our gifts is the balance process. One may be a gifted visionary but may not be good at building in the physical. A teacher in this village will be a student in another. Their teachers will be our students. Thus, we all learn together. There is an understanding of exchange in that we all give to each other. Tomorrow we will take a closer look at our community life."

We met the women just after the sunrise chanting.

One said, "We will be taking a tour of the village. We want you to see what our daily life is like here."

As we walked, we saw lots of different things going on both in different huts and in groups under the trees.

She continued: "This is my hut. I live here with my mother, my grandmother, one sister, and my mate. We have two children who are presently living with relatives in a different village. The women in my family are mostly visionaries, so I spend some time each day working with that art. I also like to cook and spend time in food preparation as my daily living activity. My mate is good at fixing things and he has spent considerable time in the South village studying construction from the builders. He is also a gifted artist, creating paintings and wood carvings."

Don't you get kind of crowded all living in the same hut?

"No. We like each other and, besides, the hut is used mainly for sleeping. There are many beautiful places outside to be, even in the rainy season."

We passed groups that were weaving and creating pottery and baskets. There were gardens of flowers, vegetables, and grains with workers busy tending them. There were groups who were engaged in some kind of schooling also. The children seemed to be intermixed with the adults, in many cases working with them. The very young children played near their mothers. I said that it seemed as though everyone was together all the time. I would miss having some alone-time.

"There is plenty of opportunity for alone-time," she said. "There are many huts out away from the village where people can spend as long as they want alone. Let's take a walk out there."

We left the village and walked on a path that went out through the jungle and came to a hut that was in a gorgeous setting by a clear stream.

"No one is using this right now, so you can take a look around."

The hut was small with a sleeping area and fire pit. Outside there were benches and places to sit by the stream.

I said I think I would like to live here.

She laughed and said, "No, you would enjoy our company in the village after a while. There are many huts like this scattered through the jungle where people can come to be alone for as long as they wish. There are also some smaller shelters farther up in the hills. Some come for a short time and some spend many days here, but the shelters are available to all. Let's head back to the village. I need to do some food preparation for our meal together, and I hope you will join us to enjoy our company."

We headed back and when we reached the village, the woman who had been talking left us. I went with the rest to an open area in the center of the village where food was already being put out. Each person took a wooden bowl and sampled the delicious variety of foods. Groups sat under trees and on benches, talking while they ate.

I said to Tinacu that I was enjoying the community here, but there didn't seem to be much that I didn't already know about community. I asked what was different here.

She said, "What is different is that all of these people really value each other as well as themselves."

I looked around and realized that I don't think I have ever been in such a large group, or perhaps not in any group at all where that had been the case.

"The women, the men, the elders, the children—everyone is equally and truly valued."

I could see that it was true. After eating and talking for a while in different groups, the instruments came out and a dance began.

The woman whom I had talked to earlier came over and said, "I forgot to tell you that we also spend part of each day playing."

Tinacu said to meet here tomorrow and we would journey together to the South village.

I met Tinacu in the East village and she suggested we take my horse to the South village. We flew along the path which was close to the ocean in most places.

"You can see there are many more retreat huts along the ocean between the villages. The difference between here and where you come from is that here anyone can use these retreat places, not just people who are rich and powerful."

How do you have enough for everyone?

"First, they are shared. There is no ownership and most people do not spend large amounts of time away from the villages. Second, our population is not larger than the land can support. We have children with care."

We came to the South village which looked much the same as the East village.

"We will talk to some women here also about what is done in this village of construction."

We walked over to a group of women who were working together, and one began describing to me what goes on there.

"We make things which have various uses and try to improve them so that they are most functional, like the bench you are sitting on. It has been improved to give more support to your back when you sit."

I agreed that it was more comfortable than other benches I have sat on.

"When we develop something new or make anything, for that matter, we must ask two questions. One is whether it is really needed. We will not make new benches just to make them, but only when old ones need replacing. The other question is whether the item has integrity."

What do you mean by "integrity"?

"It is a question both of its value—how necessary it is—and whether it can be made without violating the laws of good relationship with the environment. Sometimes, things are made here and transported to other villages, but more often one of us travels to other villages to teach them to make what they need and

164

to help them organize the production of it. Sometimes, they will send someone here to learn and then take that knowledge back to their communities."

Do you also honor the sunrise here?

"No, that is the responsibility of the East village. We do our ceremonies each day when the Sun is highest in the Sky. It is almost time for that now."

People began coming from all directions as a gong sounded out, and they gathered in the village circle. They formed a circle and began chanting and dancing together. It was quite beautiful to watch. When they were done, they ate a meal together and sat to talk with each other awhile before returning to their work.

The women showed me around the village. There were many different things being made—baskets, benches, huts, clothing, blankets, sitting mats, toys, and cooking utensils, to name a few. Everyone seemed happy in their work, some teaching, some learning.

Tinacu said that we should meet here tomorrow and then travel on to the West village.

*   *   *   *   *

Tinacu hopped on behind me and we headed for the West village, passing more retreat huts along the way. The terrain was hilly in this part of the island. We arrived around midday, and the pace seemed very leisurely.

"The West village has the responsibility of dreaming. Do you notice the different energy feeling in each village even though they look much the same?"

Now that she mentioned it, there was a distinct difference in the vibrational feeling.

"This difference in energy is maintained by the rituals which are done daily in relation to the purpose of the village."

A woman came over and introduced herself and then began to talk about their daily life.

"Our time for ceremony is at sunset, since at that time we are closest to being in the dream state. After our group ritual, we each do individual rituals and quiet time before sleeping. Our meal together is breakfast, since that is the time for sharing our dreams with each other. We have many ways we use dreaming, from dream interpretation of our inner process to lucid dreaming for changing things.

"On the full Moon we do group dreaming. Everyone living here sets an intention during our evening ceremony to dream for the community. A group creates a dream circle in the community center to hold the energy and focus of the dreaming. The next day, we have community meetings to see the implication of the dream messages for how we function as a community.

"We also do some beginning shamanic work, although that is done much more in the North village. As you continue your journey, you will see more clearly that part of the educational process here is to move from village to village, learning and balancing one's being. Visioning is followed by construction, or making one's vision real. Construction, which is very outward, is followed by dreaming, which is very inward, and dreaming is followed by wisdom and healing. Even though we have natural gifts in one area, we try to be well-balanced within ourselves."

Tinacu added, "One difference between your world and what is done here is where the emphasis is placed. Here, it is the gifts and the growth process which are most important. Other things are secondary in their support of these priorities. Here, for example, dreaming and the evolutionary development it brings are most important. Everything else that is done—building, working in the fields, preparing food—is done in support of that process."

Yes, that is very different. Dreaming in my world is seen as not very important. In comparison, my culture seems to be more like a totally unbalanced South village—construction with no vision to guide it, no dreaming to balance it, and no wisdom to heal it.

"Ah," said Tinacu, "you are beginning to see why you are here. Tomorrow we will travel on to the North village."

We met in the West village and then flew along the path near the coast to the North village. What seemed different about this village is the age of the people. The majority were older, some were middle-aged, and there were very few children. We met with some women, and one of them began to explain.

"Those who live here on a more permanent basis are people who have already learned and lived in the other three villages. We are masters of ceremony and are working on our healing skills. We work with ceremony around Sun changes, such as equinox and solstice, as well as changes in life processes. Some of us are midwives to those being born into this life, and others are midwives to those leaving this life and being born into others. We do ceremonies for those coming of age and those moving into wisdom years. We practice many healing skills, such as shamanic work, herbalism, energy healing, visualization, music, dance, and so forth.

"Our daily life has more variety than other villages, since some of us were originally East people, some South, and some West. Even those who showed early talents for healing work have lived in all the villages. So, some of us rise early with an honoring of the Sun, some stop midday to admire its brightness, and some honor its setting and entry into the Dreamtime. What we all do together is follow the rhythm of the Moon, gathering at new and full Moons for ceremony and celebration.

"Many of us travel to the other villages to teach healing and to do healing and ceremonial work. People also come here to learn. Many from other villages who are of wisdom age come here to learn and then return to live in their villages to continue their previous work but, in addition, to bring healing and ceremonial skills to their people. Some of us also serve on the council in the Central village where our wisdom is highly regarded in decision making.

"Primarily, in all that we do, honoring and learning from spirit is our focus. We recognize that the healing and wisdom come from

167

spirit, not from us, and from that place we see our connection to the whole universe."

Tinacu said we should meet here tomorrow to journey to the Central village.

*   *   *   *   *

I picked up Tinacu in the North village and we rode Cloud Dancer rather than flying to the Central village. It seemed hilly there and I think there was a lake nearby. The village was arranged like a large Medicine Wheel with paths running to the four directions. There were also small clusters of huts in each of the four directions.

Tinacu said, "The people who represent each of the villages live in the cluster of huts which is at the end of the path which leads to their village. Some people live here for long periods of time, and others come only for short stays. The representatives are chosen in each village by consensus. Other individuals are here as observers, particularly if there are multiple interests to be represented. Still others are here to learn or, in the case of elders, to provide wisdom."

We walked into the center of the village and saw a large stone plaza in a circular form with a thatched roof over the innermost part of the circle. It was beautiful stone work and there were gardens and flowers all around.

"This is where the council meets to talk of matters which concern all the villages. Things like relations with other countries, dealing with storm damage or crop failure, and other general concerns. This is also where four times each year on the equinox and solstice the villages all gather together in very large ceremonies and celebrations.

"The day in this Central village is varied depending on which cluster of huts you are living in. Each maintains the ritual schedule for their respective village and takes turns hosting group gatherings for meals. Of course, there is always a time for play

168

together. As in the other villages, each person has a daily task to fulfill in support of community living, and there are retreat areas nearby.

"The Council operates on a consensus basis, and if consensus cannot be reached, the task is not undertaken. When one or two are keeping a consensus from being reached, others from that village may be consulted to determine if they are representing the village or themselves. It is important to remember that in the consensus process, everyone's view is heard and taken seriously prior to the formulation of a plan."

Is there anything more that I should know about this village?

"It is not the particulars of this culture that are important to you, but the community process. Communities must be formed in your world, and the essentials of this community provide a good model of what works. This community structure remained successful here over a long period of time until the invasion.

"The things that are most important are that each person has a valuable gift to offer the community, and each person contributes through her or his daily tasks to support everyone else. No one is set up as better or on a higher level than anyone else. We are all learning together and what we contribute will vary with our own growth process, our age, and our interests. Time for eating together, doing ritual together, and playing together must be set aside on a daily basis. There is no competition, only cooperation. Retreat time for everyone is important and maintaining zero population growth is critical to assure that each person has equal access to food, shelter, and the joy of living, while maintaining balance with the environment. You have had an opportunity to observe this in operation here, and this will give you a greater understanding of how to put this into practice in your own world. Tomorrow we will meet back at the tipi."

I went to the tipi, entered, and sat by the door.

Mariah said, "So, you have now met and learned from all eight of these Wise Women. This last journey was different from what you expected, yet a very important lesson. You must create community in your work, and this has been an opportunity to see a functioning community in action.

"You are absolutely right in observing that all of the different communities you have interacted with during your journeys with us have been similar to the one you just encountered. There were many places all over Earth where tribal people found the recipe for successful community. Their downfall was not from a flawed community structure, but rather from being invaded by other cultures where community had run amuck, and competition, domination, and the value of material wealth over spirit became the guiding principles. It is time to reclaim our gentler ways of being with each other, where there is value for the spirit in each other and all things. You need to find ways to bring these principles of community you have learned here into the groups of people with whom you interact.

"We want to teach you the song and dance of the Grandmothers of the Wind as you become part of our community."

All the women formed a circle and began to sing and dance in a very joyous way. The song went like this:

> Grandmother, sing the wind
> Grandmother, dance the wind
> Grandmother, ride the wind
> Grandmother, call the wind
> To blow through my life
> To sweep my heart clean
> To quiet my mind
> To teach me the dance of the soul.

Mariah told me to practice it on my own. She then called me over to her and said I needed another adjustment of my crystals.

170

She checked them all. The belly was glowing a bright red-orange but seemed okay. The third eye and crown chakra needed a little tuning.

"Tomorrow, come back here, and you and I will journey together."

9

Lessons from the Past

I went to the tipi and entered.

Mariah came over and said, "Finally I get a ride on your horse!"

We went out, mounted, and flew to the West out over the ocean. We came to where Hawaii now stands, but it looked very different. There was a large village near where we landed.

"The area where this village is still remains in your time as part of Hawaii. The rest of what you see here eventually sank under the ocean. Pele helped create what has become known as Hawaii. This land, however, was called Lemuria. My people are very peaceful and balanced. Some see this culture as matriarchal, but it is only more balanced, honoring the unique gifts of both men and women. It seems woman-centered only in relation to your own culture.

"You are here for two reasons. One is to understand the influence of past lives on where you are now, and the other is to complete your initiation into the Grandmothers of the Wind. The other Grandmothers will join us here later for that.

"Let's start by talking a little about past lives. The details of those lives are not particularly important, but the lessons learned and the lessons created by them help to form the landscape of your

173

current life. You have come many times to Earth to experience human form, and you have also lived elsewhere in other parts of the Universe. The Earth walks are important to remember, for they shape the lessons for your life now. Remembering your experiences in other parts of the Universe helps you to let go of the limits which you have created by being in this human form.

"Where we are now, you experience no limits—we fly through the air on a horse with wings to a place that existed thousands of years before the lifetime you are now in. Yet when you go back to your body and life, you perceive the limits existing again. It is important to understand that those limits exist only in your perception for the purpose of learning. A greater understanding of past lives helps to transcend the limits which you have created in your current life.

"Tomorrow we will talk about a way of remembering what you need to know."

*   *   *   *   *

Mariah began talking again about past lives.

"There are two influences which are sometimes confused. One is the collective consciousness of the past. This of course influences you, since it is part of the universal mind. But it is different from the actual memory of past life experience which is attached to your soul. For example, a person would not have had to directly experience the witch burnings to have a memory of that persecution. It is so prevalent in the collective consciousness that anyone could tap into it and learn from it. That is how humanity evolves and changes as a result of experience. The individual past life experience, however, exists for the evolution of the soul which, in turn, then adds to the evolution of the whole."

How do you know whether a memory is one of collective consciousness or past life experience?

"Both will affect you in your life. So far, you have remembered things about your past lives because of fears or understandings present in your current life that have no particular experience in

174

this life to which they could be attributed. These individual past life experiences usually carry very strong emotion. More general awareness, without such strong emotion, is often from the collective unconscious. When intentionally working on past life issues, the first part of the process is to move into the place where your soul lives. Do you understand what I mean by that?"

I think I do. There is a place I have constructed inside where I go to do healing work, and I would say that when I am there, I am aligned with my soul or coming from the place of my soul.

"Yes, that is correct. So, while you are there, you ask for your soul guide to come—not the guide for this particular life—but your soul guide. When the guide appears, ask to be shown a previous life which contains lessons for your current life. Let's try this once now and see what comes. Sit in a comfortable spot and move into that space."

I sat under a tree near the beach and pictured my inner place. There are many beautiful things in this space. I started into the tipi where the tools for healing which I often use were neatly arranged. But I sensed that I was to go out by the river. I sat where the water was running fast, and I could see the mist from the falls up river. I asked for my soul guide to come. Then I felt a presence of light to the right of me.

I kept trying to see it, and a voice said, "What are you doing?"

I am trying to see you clearly.

The voice said, "You don't need to see me. Just feel me."

So I asked to see a previous lifetime which had a lesson for me.

"Well, let's start in Lemuria. You lived here at a time when humans here were very well developed in their abilities to manifest and create their realities. The people remembered that they were creators. From the time you were a child, you were raised with this understanding, and life was peaceful and happy.

"When you were a young woman, other humans came here who did not remember their original instructions. They came with news of wars and natural disasters. Some of the people said, 'Well, it doesn't have to be that way. We can change that,' but others said,

'But it is that way. These people have seen it.' And a division began among the people which, in turn, created a division in the Earth. A large part of Lemuria sank into the ocean, while new land was pushed up. You and some others remained on the part that stayed.

"While at the time you understood your new creation, over time you and the others began to think that this was something that could 'just happen' to you, and you feared what the future might bring. The lesson you are struggling to learn in your current life is that destiny is only fear of the future and predictions from the past."

That sounded so profound that I felt it to be true, but I couldn't quite grasp the meaning. I moved back into the space with Mariah.

She said, "You must work with this method on your own. We will continue talking about this tomorrow."

* * * * *

I met Mariah, and she asked about the lesson from my soul guide yesterday and whether I had any questions.

I said that I was still contemplating the statement that destiny is only fear of the future and predictions from the past.

She said, "'Destiny' in the sense used here is about the happenings in your life, not your soul path. It is about the way many humans create their lives without awareness, bringing to themselves the things which they believe or fear will happen, so that they may learn from them. As you learn, you begin to become more aware of what you are creating. With even greater awareness, you learn how you are creating. At that point, you begin to make conscious decisions about what you will create.

"You have a question in your mind about what it would be like to be a conscious creator in each moment. Let's look at what creation without awareness is. Predictions from the past would be thoughts such as 'It's always been this way,' 'This is just human nature,' or 'I could never do that.' And so it is. Fear of the future

would be thoughts such as 'I'd better be careful or…' and 'What if I get sick, injured, don't have enough money?' And so it is.

"As one who creates from awareness, peaceful thoughts are used to create a peaceful life. Moving into the vibration of health keeps you healthy or restores health. Focusing thought and feeling on that which you want creates it. Thoughts and feelings of worthiness create abundance. When you are coming from the place of your soul, or a centeredness, as opposed to fears or past expectations, what you want leads you further on your soul journey, while fears and expectations create blocks to that journey. Why don't you go to your soul place and ask your soul guide about another past life?"

I went and sat where I had been yesterday, moved to my soul place to find my soul guide, and asked to see another past life. The guide showed me one of which I was already aware.

"This is the life where you were raised by your grandmother. She was teaching you medicine ways, and because your life ended early, she never finished. She has been completing that work with you in this life, as you are aware. The lesson comes from how you died. A mate wanted you to go with him to live in another village some distance away. You did not want to leave your grandmother and refused to go with him. He decided to take you along against your will, and in the struggle, you were killed. Possessiveness is a quality you fear. You behave in ways now that do not allow others to possess you, although many you have called to you in your current life wish to do so. Your fear calls to them."

I realized that was true, but it was not clear how to let go of this fear. I came back to where Mariah was and she said I should journey as often as I can with my new schedule.

*　　*　　*　　*　　*

Mariah was waiting and continued talking about past lives.

"After you have worked with this technique awhile, you will encounter past lives which have been somewhere other than on Earth. It is important to be aware that the purpose of remembering these past experiences is to become more conscious of the lessons in your present life. In the case of lives elsewhere in the Universe, you will gain a greater perspective on the purpose of your current life."

I think you lost me somewhere back on the idea of learning to be the creator of my life. I have been thinking quite a bit about that and have many questions. For example, if I create, with or without awareness, everything that happens in my experience, then how do I explain something like my horse cutting his leg this morning? It was in my experience, so does that mean I created it? Or suppose someone close to me was injured. It is in my experience, so did I create it? I can certainly see how I create many things, but I'm not sure I understand it all.

"I'm glad you have been contemplating this. First, I will answer that, yes, you do create everything you experience. When the creation is without awareness, you would naturally not see the connection. You have feelings about the horse which become manifest. The connection between you and the horse allowed the manifestation to occur. It is no different than your manifestations from conscious awareness—the wind coming up when you sing to it, the Thunder Beings bringing rain when you call, the healing work that you do. The only difference is in your awareness.

"If an injury came to someone you know, you and that person become part of each other's manifestation in that each of you is creating your own experience. There is no blame or judgment about what you have created, for it is only an opportunity to gain conscious awareness of yourself as the creator."

I think I'll have to contemplate this a little more.

"It is a little like putting together a puzzle. The pieces which you understand fit together and show you a little bit of the picture. There are many other pieces whose shapes and colors don't even

seem to belong to that puzzle, yet in the end they will all form a coherent picture. Let's do one more past life journey and then tomorrow we will move on to other things."

I sat again and moved to the place of my soul. My soul guide came and I asked to see another past life with a lesson for me. Again, it was a life I was already somewhat aware of, one in which I appeared as a woman in my forties in Europe. It was at a time when the old ways were being stamped out by Christianity. I saw myself in a yard behind a cottage where I was feeding animals and picking herbs to bring in to dry. I smiled as I walked into the cottage which smelled of herbs drying. It seemed that I worked as a midwife and herbalist for the small village where I lived. When I went in, there were men in my cottage and herb containers broken on the floor. They grabbed me and tied my hands behind my back. I heard them killing my animals outside. In a trial, I was asked what I did and I told them I was a midwife and prepared herbs. They said I was a witch. I said it was a gift, and they burned me. I asked my soul guide what the lesson was for me now.

"In that life, you chose to die rather than hide your gifts and not use them. It was a courageous but painful death. Pain has a way of making one reconsider courage. It is important for you to remember that it was your choice, and that the courage to give your gifts in the face of opposition is still important, and almost as important as the question of whether you need to create the opposition. I'll let you ponder that."

At the moment, my brain felt like mush just thinking about that last statement. I went back to where Mariah was waiting and told her that I had enough past life lessons to keep my head spinning for some time.

"Good," she said. "As you begin to integrate these lessons, there will be many more. Tomorrow we will move on to other topics."

Good, I said.

*   *   *   *   *

Mariah and I walked through the village and came to a stone plaza in the center of which was a very large and beautiful crystal.

I asked where it came from and she said, "The stories say that it was a gift long ago from the star people."

I said that it looked like a star itself the way it glowed.

"It captures the sunlight by day and the moon and starlight at night," she said.

"We are headed to the North end of this island where there is a ceremonial place for women."

We arrived at a very beautiful, black sand beach and walked up to rocks in which there was an opening. As we stepped into a cave, I could hear water running. After moving through the dimly lit passageway, we came to an open space where the Sun was shining through the ceiling on a small waterfall within the cave. Off to the other side was a deep pool. The Sun on the black rock walls sparkled like stars in the night. I said that this could not be more beautiful if it had been planned.

"The Mother is an incredible artist," she said.

We walked back out to the beach and sat down.

"This is where we will complete your initiation into the Wise Woman phase of your life and your initiation into the circle of the Grandmothers of the Wind. The other Grandmothers will join us here tomorrow."

Why are we doing this initiation in Lemuria?

"Because all of us had lives here except for our oldest Grandmother. She was a teacher here for a period of time, however, and wished to continue teaching with us as part of the circle. You also had a lifetime here and will join us as a teacher as well. This will take some time, since we still have much to tell you, and you will need some alone-time to find your own wisdom. Tomorrow we will begin."

When I arrived on the black sand beach, there were huts set up along the tree line. There was lots of chatter and activity. Mariah came up to me, and I commented that this was such a beautiful place to set up camp! I noticed a large circle drawn in the sand in front of the entrance to the cave. The other Grandmothers of the wind gathered round, and Mariah said we would go up the hill to a place on top of the cave.

As we all started up the path, which was rather steep, it seemed odd to have all the Grandmothers here in this new place. When we got to the top, there was a circle of stones out on the cliff overlooking the beach and ocean. We could also see a great distance to the South, including much of the island. We sat inside the stones on the outer perimeter of the circle, each in our usual directions. Mariah began to speak.

"As you know, we call ourselves Grandmothers of the Wind or Wise Women of the Wind, and we are teachers of change. You are also a teacher and will join us. You have taught many things in your life, and you have observed each of us in the teacher role, so now it is time to explore what you will be teaching as part of our circle and as you move into the Wise Woman place. In making the commitment to join us, you are also committing to living your life with the highest integrity and being a conscious creator of your life.

"It is time now for you to go by yourself into the cave where the waterfall is to listen for your wisdom. We would like you to go there now, and when you come back tomorrow, go directly to that spot and stay there. Continue to return there until you have found what you are seeking and then come out to meet us on the beach in front of the cave. The easiest way to the cave is down the same path we came up."

I went back down the path and entered the large hole in the rocks. I walked through the darkness until I came to the place where the Sun was shining down on the falls. I sat down for a moment and then decided to bathe in the pool. I took off my clothes and slipped into the still, black water, washing away all the old parts of me that I no longer needed. My old life and limiting beliefs and thoughts sank down into the depths of the dark pool. After climbing out, I sat on the smooth, black rock which sparkled like a night Sky full of stars. The waterfall was on my right, and the dark, still pool on my left. The Sun shifted so that it was shining directly on me, drying off the remaining drops of water, and warming my body and the black rock which surrounded me. I knew it was time to leave, and I anticipated coming back to see what visions this cave held for me.

*   *   *   *   *

I flew to the black sand beach in front of the cave and entered. When I reached the place by the waterfall and pool, I decided I needed to go into the pool again to let go of the limiting thoughts running through my mind. I took off my clothes and slipped into the water, letting all limits sink to the bottom. I climbed out and lay on the smooth, sparkling black rock to dry in the sunlight. I felt the quiet depths of the dark pool on my left and the brightness of the moving water on my right.

I looked around the cave from this perspective and stated my intentions for being there: I have come to find some clarity about what I am to teach in this phase of my life.

I waited and paid attention to what came through my mind. Certainly it was working with women's transitions, particularly through menopause. Then I thought of what I would teach when I was one of the Grandmothers of the Wind. It seemed as if the Grandmothers had covered everything.

Then there was a voice which said, "You need to teach about the physical changes during moonpause."

But, I said, there are many books and teachings on that already.

"You will teach about the physical changes, not from a physical viewpoint, but from the perspective of all that the Grandmothers of the Wind have taught you."

182

Oh, I said, that would be different. It would take some work to put that together, but it would be an exciting thing to think about.

"The Grandmothers have taught you about spirit and energy systems on many levels. The physical changes in a woman's body must be seen in that light. It will give a new way of seeing how they might be experienced and understood."

I was still contemplating that when the voice began again.

"Another thing you will teach is about social change, how to move toward a society which is more fully human—where spirit is embodied more fully."

What would I have to say about social change that is new?

"It is not new information as much as it is seeing from a new perspective. Again, if you apply what the Grandmothers have taught you, you will see how many change efforts might be different. Wise Women are always agents of social change because they hold the energy of good relationship and spin the webs of greater conscious awareness for their people."

I said I'd have to think about that one a bit too.

"Your dance is of the bridge between Earth and Sky, the physical and the spiritual. Does it not fit then that you would teach how to work on the physical plane from a spiritual perspective?"

I could see that it was true. I knew that I was to come back again tomorrow for more information.

*   *   *   *   *

I worked on trying to really be in the cave rather than just seeing myself there. I bathed in the pool, and many more limiting thoughts slipped to the bottom. Somehow, they seem to come back when I am going through my daily activities, but I shed them now as a snake sheds its skin. As I dried on the smooth, black rock in the sunlight, I was aware of the energy of the water on my right and the deep stillness of the pool on my left.

I said to the cave and rocks and water that I was back to learn more about what I am to teach. A voice began a review of yesterday's revelations.

"You are to teach women about the physical changes which occur in their bodies, but from the perspective of what has been taught to you by the Grandmothers. You will also teach how to change your communities from this perspective. Both are very important for your world right now. Women must learn to assume their power and wisdom as they grow older to create the needed changes in the ways humans are living in relationship to each other and Earth."

I understand this from what was said yesterday and I see why this is important, but is there more?

"A third thing you will teach also deals with gaining wisdom, and it is how to let go of limitations and become a conscious creator. Older women must assume their role as wisdom keepers in your society, and the wisdom which is necessary to teach is the understanding and remembering of the role humans have as creators."

Well, I think I can teach the first two things with some work on my part, but to teach others about their role as creator when I am only beginning to understand that myself seems a little overwhelming.

"One always teaches best what one is also actively learning. The knowledge and wisdom will continue to grow as you continue to learn and teach. Remember that we all are learning on many levels, and all you are ever asked to teach is what you know. Besides, you are only teaching how to find one's own wisdom. All three things you must prepare to teach as you move into the next stage of your life. Go now out onto the beach where your sisters are waiting for you."

I expressed my gratefulness to the cave and went through the darkness out onto the beach. It was evening, and Mariah took me for a ritual bathing to a place where the water from the cave tumbled out of the rocks. The women gathered around to welcome me back.

Mariah said, "Tomorrow you should not journey, but contemplate what you have learned. Then the next three days, we will be here on the beach in preparation and ceremony."

*   *   *   *   *

The Grandmothers were waiting on the black sand beach, sitting around the circle which had been drawn in the sand. The place at the East was open for me. I took my place between Grandmother on my right and Tinacu on my left. Mariah asked if I had contemplated what I had learned in the cave.

Yes, I said. Teaching the first thing—physical changes through moonpause from your perspectives—seems the most possible, although I do not yet grasp exactly what I will teach. The second thing—teaching social action from a new perspective—I really am not quite sure about. Tinacu teaches how communities can function well, so it's not that.

"What we haven't taught you and what you will learn to teach is how to create the change in your world which is necessary to get to the place that Tinacu teaches about," said Mariah.

Well, I said, I'm not sure how to do that yet, let alone teach it. The third thing—teaching how to be the conscious creator of one's life—I don't know how to do well either. I feel as if I might be like a first grader teaching a kindergartner how to read.

"We each must learn one step at a time, and who can be a better teacher for one learning a step than one who has just taken it? You are not really teaching information, but about a new way of being. You were told at the beginning of your spiritual journey by a group of Grandmothers that the way to teach is to be what you are teaching, and that is still true.

"What all three of these areas have in common is that they require the merging of spirit with the physical. Seeing the physical changes from a spiritual perspective and approaching social change from a spiritual standpoint lead directly to the understanding of yourself as creator. Bridging the physical and spiritual in a way that removes the artificial separation between

185

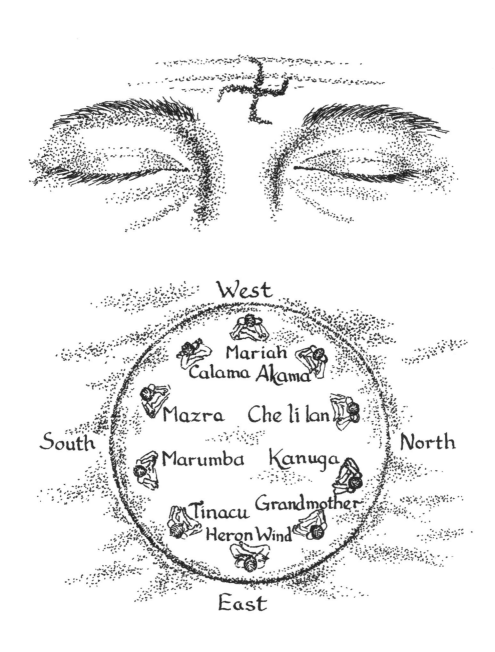

West

Mariah
Calama Akama

Mazra   Che li lan

South   North

Marumba   Kanuga

Tinacu   Grandmother
Heron Wind

East

Grandmothers of the Wind

186

them is what you have chosen to teach with us. Let's dance together to the song we taught you."

All the women began dancing to the Grandmothers of the Wind song as the wind blew off the water and over our circle. Mariah then called me over and traced a reverse swastika on my forehead with her finger.

"Remember when we painted you at the beginning of our journey together? The symbol we use has many meanings and all of them are about motion. The movement of the Sun, the Moon, the Earth, and the wind—all are cycles of change. Another name for us could be Grandmothers of Change, since all of our teachings are about changes as we grow in consciousness together. We welcome you to this circle as our sister.

"Our identities are ones we have chosen from lives which allow us to most easily teach the lessons we offer. The identity on a soul level, of course, is much larger than a single lifetime. You, as well, may choose which lifetime you will take your teaching identity from."

I think that since I am teaching things which are relevant in my current lifetime, I need to take that identity. At least for now.

"Even though we assume the identity of a particular life, we all draw on our soul learning and experience in all that we teach."

* * * * *

The women were sitting around the circle on the beach again. I got really present there, sensing the directions and seeing it all clearly from a sense of my body being there. I then walked over and sat in my place in the East.

Mariah said, "We thought we would give you a chance to ask questions about us."

Well, there are so many questions, I don't know where to begin. How did this group come together and how did each of you get here?

"This circle has been in existence for a very long time. I said to you before that what we all have in common is a lifetime in

Lemuria. We did not all know each other then, since we were here at different times over a long span of years, but we are all committed to the values and truths we understood here.

"All of us came to this circle much the same way as you have. Although not all of us are currently operating out of an Earth walk, we have all chosen on a soul level to teach certain truths which must be kept alive through the Wise Women and Grandmothers. In some ways, you might think of us as the University in the Sky, since we preserve the important and universal teachings over cultures and time. In other ways, we are quite different from a university as you know it. We understand that our students are very gifted and can teach us many things too. We all enhance each other's conscious growth.

"As I said, we have been in existence as a circle for a very long time, but not with all the souls you see here now. Each of us has our own soul path, and being part of this circle for a period of time is on our journey. We each must leave at some point to continue on our paths of evolvement. Someone left before you came, leaving the space in the East open for you."

I guess that answers most of the questions I am able to formulate at this time.

"Each of us has lived what we teach, and you will live what you teach also. Come over to me and we will officially make you part of this circle."

I walked over to Mariah and she placed around my neck a necklace with the reverse swastika on it. The arms of the swastika were each in a different color—red, black, white, and yellow. As I looked around the circle, each woman wore a similar necklace. Each necklace seemed to be unique, constructed with different materials, but all bearing the symbol of the multicolored swastika.

"This is the symbol of the Grandmothers of the wind. It represents, as we said before, movement and cycles, and the colors represent the different peoples of the world as they are represented in this circle. It includes everything and everyone. You are now a part of our circle, a Grandmother of the Wind, and we will be teaching you more about this role in the days to come.

"Now I want to readjust your crystals again." She adjusted the third eye and crown chakra crystals.

"Spend some time today finding a song to represent your understanding of limitlessness and being a creator. Tomorrow we will complete your instructions for the next step."

I then moved around the circle hugging each of my sisters and teachers—Akama, Che li lan, Kanuga, Grandmother, Tinacu, Marumba, Mazra, Calama, and back to Mariah. The music began and we all danced to the Grandmothers of the Wind song. The dolphins jumped in the ocean next to us, and the wind blew through our hair as we danced our joyful dance.

*   *   *   *   *

When I arrived at the beach, I quickly moved to my place in the circle.

Mariah said, "Did you find the song?"

I said I found it while I was walking last night, but it makes me laugh to sing it.

"Why do you laugh when you sing it?"

For two reasons, I guess. One is that the melody sounds like a theme song from a Disney movie, and the other is that what the song says seems impossible to do. The reasons are probably related, in that Disney movies are flights of the imagination, and what the song says seems more imagined than real.

"That's very appropriate then, since it is through our imaginations that we create. If we cannot imagine something, then we cannot consciously create it. Let's hear your song."

I sang:

> I am creator of my experience
> I am creator of my life.
> I move in conscious awareness of the possibilities
> From which I choose in each moment.

"You are right. It makes me smile to hear it also. It is a good affirmation to help you create with happy feelings. Let's all sing it."

All the women began singing with me, smiling as they sang.

"Your next step is to write about the three areas you have chosen to teach. Work on each section by itself in the order it came to you—physical changes, social action, and becoming a conscious creator. The best way to begin may be to just sit and write. You might want to review what each of us has taught you as it relates to the subject, particularly with the first two areas. You may journey to the tipi to discuss any of it with us whenever you wish. After you have completed a section, come to talk with us there. This will not be as difficult to accomplish as you now think. Keep singing your song to make you smile as you create. Let's all sing and dance together before you leave this place."

I will miss it here. It is so beautiful!

The women began singing the creator song together using "we" instead of "I." Then we moved into dancing the Grandmothers of the Wind song as the wind came up and the dolphins surfaced in the water nearby.

I went to my horse, mounted, and flew home.

10

Weaving the Wisdom, Creating the Power

As the Grandmothers instructed, I began to write about the three areas which I am to teach. As I became clearer on each one, I looked at each from the perspective of all that the Grandmothers have taught me. The following is what emerged.

The Physical Changes

At menopause, a woman is moving into the third phase of her life, and during this time, there are many changes and adjustments which occur in her body. This is not surprising considering the adjustments which occurred when she moved from childhood into womanhood. When seen as isolated events from a totally physical perspective, these body changes are often viewed as "symptoms" to be controlled or eliminated. In fact, because our culture does not value older women, there seems to be an attempt to suppress or hide any signs of aging or movement into this third phase. We are routinely given hormones to keep us young, eliminate our hot flashes, keep our vaginas moist, prevent heart attacks, and slow bone loss.

I have read in several sources that the medical world views menopause as a fairly recent event in the history of womankind, since it is only in the last two centuries that women have had a life expectancy much beyond fifty years of age. Common sense and her-story, on the other hand, would lead one to believe that even though the average life expectancy may have been low due to accident, disease, and complications in childbirth, many women lived to be quite old. There are many examples of indigenous peoples from around the world where the elders range from seventy to one hundred years old. Menopause could not have been all that rare an occurrence.

In our culture, then, menopause is seen not only as a physical event, but as a medical event to be treated. This appears to be a very limited viewpoint in light of women's own experience of this change in our own culture, other cultures, and her-story.

An alternative perspective has emerged from my work with the Grandmothers of the Wind. Their work with me has served as an initiation into what I believe is a very old tradition which bridges many cultures and spans many thousands of years of human existence. In this tradition, a woman in the third phase of her life is greatly valued and has much responsibility to the community in which she lives.

There is a process of moving into this phase with wisdom, a process which is facilitated by the elder women who have already assumed their Wise Woman roles. The physical changes which accompany the process are seen as a part of the whole self, including its physical, emotional, mental, and spiritual aspects, which is transforming at this time. A woman is taught the art of self-knowledge, self-healing, ceremony, creation, balance, and conscious awareness, all of which prepare her to assume her respected role of Wise Woman within her community.

The physical changes are part of the preparation as she learns to be aware of and move the energy within her own body. Each woman's experience of these changes is as unique as she is; her body creates the experience she needs. The reasons for each physical experience lie within each woman, not in a book or in a physician's mind. The seeking for these reasons within ourselves leads to wisdom. Thus, what is important is the process of working with these "symptoms" as teachers, not as problems to be managed. In reading nearly everything I have been able to get my hands on about alternative approaches to working with menopausal symptoms, I am struck by the wide array of treatments which seems to work for everything from hot flashes to calcium loss. These treatments include herbs, acupuncture, meditation, body work, vitamins, diet, exercise, etc., and are recommended by both practitioners of alternative health care and also by women who have made the journey themselves.

The dilemma which this creates for the woman who is beginning to experience symptoms is deciding which approach will work for her. What an interesting question. Hopefully, it is the beginning of a search which will take a woman deep into her own knowledge, so that she can listen to her body and find answers that are right for her. Discomfort is often the push we need to start the journey to wisdom.

There is no doubt that the physical cause of the symptoms we experience is related to the hormones which fluctuate over a period of years before our bleeding ceases. Being able to explain this process on a physical level does not mean that there is not also a larger explanation which also involves our emotions, our spirit, and the preparation for a new phase of life.

After moonpause, both estrogen and progesterone are low, a situation which is similar to when our bleeding begins during our monthly cycles. Both ancient wisdom and modern research suggest that this is a time when we are most open to change, most in touch with our own knowing, feeling our greatest power, and closest to spirit. In a sense, we remain in this state throughout the third phase of our lives, while during the second life phase we experience it briefly only once a month.

The fluctuation of hormones which moves us toward this time of holding our power and standing in the center of our knowing creates power surges, or hot flashes, as the energy moves up through our chakras, gaining intensity as it goes. The heat that is generated cleanses our bodies, perhaps destroying potential cancer cells which may have developed during our reproductive years and which are heat sensitive. Long periods and heavy periods often seen in menopause may serve a cleansing function, while short and skipped periods prepare us gently for assuming our power. The fibroids and other growths which sometimes appear are reflections of the blocks we still carry from our wounding as women, pointing the way to the discovery of healing for physical, emotional, and spiritual pain.

There are many times when my mind wants me to believe that when my body hurts, it is just physical, but my work with the Grandmothers has led me into a world where nothing is "just physical." Our physical bodies and their conditions are manifestations of the blocks in the energy flow. The blocks in the energy flow are due to emotional issues which have accumulated during our lives. The emotional issues are lessons constructed by our souls. The lessons are the way in which we evolve in consciousness during a lifetime.

It is sometimes difficult to convey this understanding without the issues of blame and guilt arising, creating grounds for self-criticism and judgment. We seem to have the notion in our culture that when we experience problems, either physical or emotional, we have failed, are somehow not good enough, or are being punished for something we've done.

As I understand it, none of us is perfect, or will ever become perfect, in this lifetime. We all have lessons and those lessons take on different physical forms for different people. There is no blame for creating lessons from which you can learn. This would be like blaming the teacher for giving challenging tests. Tests are ways in which we learn, and if we always performed perfectly on the test, we would not need to study that particular subject because we would have already learned it.

Lessons are also not about comparing ourselves with others to see who has learned the most or the fastest. Our journeys are unique and often are not what they appear on the surface. I cannot pretend to know what lessons the corporate executive has chosen to learn compared to those chosen by a homeless person. The only thing that I can hope to be an authority on and student of is my own experience. A great lesson occurred for me when I stopped judging myself for what I created and instead began to trust the process of growing and learning from lessons presented over a lifetime.

In considering what I would write about the physical changes in moonpause as an initiation into the Wise Woman phase, I reviewed the teachings of the Grandmothers and imagined participating in a discussion of this topic with them. The following is what I heard them say.

Akama: "I would point out that the physical experience may be a manifestation of an energy block related to shadow work. The physical points to where the shadow work needs to be done. Find the shadow associated with a particular physical problem and work with it, either letting it dissolve into the golden light to feed the fire within you or integrating it into yourself to create strength and wisdom."

Calama: "It helps to look at our bodies through our Dreamtime eyes. What we see with our physical eyes and experience with our physical senses is not all there is. As we look beyond the physical, we see the energy lines to the objects of addiction. Learn to cut them and replace them with lines of attachment to those things which truly feed our bodies and souls. We go into the darkness within ourselves and see that there is nothing to fear. Instead we find our Wise Woman living there, as wisdom lives within the darkness. The darkness represents what we have yet to learn, while the light represents what we already know. As she becomes our most trusted friend and lover, we move into the beautiful, full flower of the Wise Woman phase of awareness."

Che li lan: "I cannot stress enough the importance of doing preventative work with the energy systems of your body. Learning to be aware of and scanning on a regular basis the energy flow within your body will allow you to detect blocks on that level before they manifest into the physical. This will also remove at an early stage those blocks which are already represented in the physical. Even just attending to and moving the energy in your body daily will be helpful. It is also important for women to come together in groups to do energy healing with each other. When several are gathered together, the intensity of healing work is magnified."

Mazra: "Awareness and understanding of energy within and around us keep us healthy. Physical problems often indicate a lesson regarding the balance of energy. When we learn from the energy systems around us, which are maintained by the plant spirits, we begin to see the relationships among the systems of our bodies, the Earth, and the Universe. The plants teach us about nourishing our bodies and ourselves as women. We learn to live each day as a ceremony in good relationship with all the systems which support our existence. Trusting the deep feminine voice within us will show the way to the healing of our own bodies as well as the body of Earth."

Kanuga: "The information we need to heal our bodies comes from our heart centers. Self-healing is a daily ritual as we learn to use the light beams which come from our heart. Our hands direct them to the area of our body which needs healing, and we then visualize the problem as darkness which turns to light. The ritual we develop can create greater intensity of healing energy and can also move the energy in our bodies, thereby preventing physical problems. I agree with Che li lan that prevention should be a main focus. Drinking pure water, eating nourishing food, and getting enough rest maintain good energy flow. It is more difficult to remove a block once it has been created than it is to keep the energy moving to begin with. When we can work with the energy within us in this way, it allows us to enhance the healing effect of herbs by sensing their energy and directing that energy to the places within our bodies where it is most needed."

Marumba: "When we learn to feel the rhythms within our bodies, we can then learn to change them. Any body disturbance creates an altered rhythm. As we explore the rhythms of the physical disturbance and the emotions which accompany it, we can see our lessons clearer and restore our natural rhythms of health. Learn to dance your feelings—fears, sorrows, and joys—until you can trust your body's ability to return to its natural rhythm. When the change is made into the Wise Woman phase, the

196

rhythms become more accentuated to capture our attention, showing us the blocks which prevent us from dancing our wisdom. Pay attention to the rhythms, and dance your path to wisdom."

Grandmother: "When we create beauty around us, it must reflect the beauty within us. The human body is indeed a beautiful energy system as are the other systems of Earth. Awareness of the energy and nurturing of the system are essential, as my sisters have pointed out. Being in good relationship with all that is around us is a critical part of the process. When we eat to nourish our bodies, we need to ask whether the food was raised and harvested in good relationship and respect for the spirit of the plants or animals involved. If it was not, then we are part of that cycle of disrespect, ungratefulness, and imbalance.

"This is also an important question to ask regarding the ways in which the body is treated when physical problems arise. Whatever medication, procedure, or treatment used should be one which restores balance and good relationship, rather than disrupting them further. As an example, Heron tells me that a common medication used for women going through moonpause is made from the urine of pregnant horses who are treated like machines in a manufacturing process, with their offspring killed because they are only 'by-products' of the process. Your sisters, the horses, are dishonored by this type of treatment. You must always ask that the medications you use, the food that you eat, and the healing procedures which are used involve respect and good relationship with your brothers and sisters who support your existence on Earth. I would also suggest using regular cleansing rituals of some sort. Many aspects of your society are toxic, and cleansing rituals remove the physical, emotional, mental, and spiritual toxins from your being, allowing better health and functioning on all levels."

Tinacu: "As women come together to support each other in the transition into the Wise Woman phase, the differences in our experience should be honored. The differences in our bodies and our lessons are related to the uniqueness of our gifts. We need to

197

support each other in the process without judgment of ourselves or others. Each of us contributes to the whole of our experience at this time. If Wise Women were all identical with the same gifts and lessons, we would need no more than one woman! Instead, we weave a rich tapestry of wisdom among us, each with our own colorful threads of wisdom."

Mariah: "Sometimes the blocks we encounter in our transition during moonpause are related to issues from other lifetimes. This is a time for connecting with the soul guide for a better perspective on both the gifts and lessons associated with this Earth walk. It is a time of integrating the wisdom we have gained throughout our lives with our larger purpose on a soul level. Now we are ready to learn how to really live our lives to the fullest as we become aware of our creations and learn to create intentionally."

Heron: "When I look at how women might apply all of this wisdom to the issues they face during the moonpause transition, it is important to see this as a process. As women, we come into this awareness with varied backgrounds and experience. Some of us have come to moonpause early through surgical means, and others have physical conditions which currently warrant medical intervention. Whatever our circumstance, we begin a process of relating to our bodies as energy systems and to ourselves as the source of knowledge for our healing. To have surgery or not, to take medication or not, these are not questions to be answered by a physician or a book. They are questions to be answered by the Wise Woman within. The journey through this transition into moonpause is to find her."

Cloud Dancer was waiting, and it was good to see him again. We flew through the sky to the Grandmothers' tipi. I entered and sat by the door in the East, greeting each of the women with a nod. I told them I had finished the first part of the writing and asked if there were any changes they wished to make.

Grandmother said, "When I spoke to you about the physical changes, I also stressed the importance of doing cleansing ritual. I would like you to include that."

I said that I would. I told them that I wasn't sure how to proceed with the next section on social action and change.

Mariah said, "Use the same method you did for the part on physical changes, and it will come together. Come back to see us when you are finished with this next part."

Social Change

I think I gave up on social change when I was in my twenties. Prior to that, I was very idealistic, ready to revamp the whole world. It was working with children of migrant workers for two summers that made me think social change seemed hopeless. The "upstanding" people of the church, who I thought believed in the Golden Rule, would not shake hands with the African-American migrant workers who helped us lead their church service. After this experience, I couldn't see how I could make a difference in the efforts for social change. After about ten or fifteen years of minding my own business, I decided that the only way I could change anything was to change myself. So I worked on that diligently, trying to clean up my own little corner of the Universe—a much more difficult task than I had imagined at the start, I might add.

At this point in my life, I still believe that we can each find within us all the problems which our society and the Earth are experiencing now—from pollution to violence and destruction. It is important to deal with these issues within ourselves, so that we know them well and learn how to change them inside. As I move into the Wise Woman time, I feel the pull toward the development of community and the blending of my wisdom with that of other Wise Women to create change and to support the shift in conscious awareness which is occurring at this time.

Working with the Grandmothers of the Wind has pushed me further along a path which has been influenced by the strong women I have known who dared to step away from the traditional and expected roles and rules for women and, instead, stood in their own knowing and truth. As a Grandmother, it is now my responsibility to take social action. It is not something I must do alone, but along with other Wise Women who are finding the need to stand in their truth as well. Our way of acting will always come from balance, harmony, respect for all things, and good relationship, but we will stand firm in our knowing.

Again, I looked to the Grandmothers of the Wind for their wisdom about how social change might be accomplished in a new way—the Grandmothers' way. As I imagined sitting in circle with them, the following is what they said:

Akama: "We see the shadow within us reflected back to us in all that is around us—the rocks, the trees, the animals, each other. When you look at a situation in your society which needs changing, you must first explore what it reflects within yourself. By working with the shadow, either individual or collective, we discover the ways to change the society."

Calama: "As I have said before, things are not always as they appear in physical form. Look beyond the individual behaviors to be changed or issues to be addressed and move to a greater awareness with your Dreamtime vision. See the spiritual and energy relationships that exist and need to be addressed. Doing so will produce lasting change."

Che li lan: "Teach people about the energy systems in their bodies. This awareness will facilitate the interaction of those working for change. Maintaining a body free of energy blocks will enhance your effectiveness in bringing about change."

Mazra: "Gather people together to do ceremony around social change issues. These ceremonies should be designed to bring about an awareness of how important each individual is in creating a healthy Universe. Become beneficial parasites on the Earth Mother. Learn from the flowers and animals about the natural balance of things so that your goals in social change restore harmony in the Universe as well as in your own hearts."

Kanuga: "Healing in your society must be directed by your own hearts. This requires a shift in the power structure to make the individual the authority in healing. The healer or physician's role is only to support the self-healing process. This is also a model for social change. Change requires that the group support each individual's growth process."

Marumba: "When you want to change how people are dancing, change the rhythm. Change it slowly so everyone can keep up. Create new rhythms which synchronize with the whole. Dance the rhythm of peace and love in your life so that all around you feel the vibrations. When you do this, all the Universe dances with you."

Grandmother: "A grandmother holds the power of creation in her belly and uses that power wisely. The power to change things comes from walking, talking, and standing firm in one's truth. A grandmother speaks in a loving but firm way about the violations of good relationship and teaches respect for all things to those who need to learn. In words of your time, the grandmother 'tells it like it is,' seeing through the masks of separation which your society has created. Grandmothers will lead the way in social change."

Tinacu: "The model of community which I have shown you is also the structure for any group wishing to take social action. As you gather grandmothers together, create community among you so that your power unites with the energy of the Universe, energizing the change process. Honor each other's gifts and journeys. Create a many-colored tapestry in which you can wrap the issues in a bundle to create change in beauty."

Mariah: "Our individual and collective experiences of the past converge on the present change efforts. We draw from our lessons to create new possibilities, new ways of being. The awareness of ourselves as spirit allows us to manifest into the physical the beauty of our wholeness. Social change is created out of this awareness and our understanding of our relatedness which comes with it. Anything is possible. As Wise Women, we chose from these possibilities to create a world of beauty, joy, peace, and love."

Heron: "It is so difficult for me to imagine working from this perspective in most of the social situations I encounter in this culture, because they tend to function on a purely physical level. Yet it becomes increasingly difficult to pretend that the other dimensions are not real or important. While I am not exactly sure how to go about acting from this other perspective, I know that I will. It feels a little like imagining something which I have not seen before. I get little glimpses of pieces which continue to expand into the whole.

"I have also felt this way about developing community, because I believe that very few, if any, of us have ever really experienced a functional community, while at the same time we are being called to develop this way of living together. So I will continue to focus on the little pieces which I can see clearly, trusting that the picture will grow as my consciousness and awareness expand. A number of individuals from my women's circle have been inducted into the Grandmother Lodge, and it seems as if that is a good place to start practicing our wisdom together. We will turn our collective vision, dreams, and truth to the creation of social change, leading the way to the future as Wise Women."

I felt Cloud Dancer's sleek coat and the power beneath me as once again I flew through the Sky to the tipi in the clouds. I entered and took my place in the East. I greeted them all and said that I was done with the second part of my writing. Mariah asked how I liked it. I said that I guess it is okay, but I have difficulty writing about something I haven't done yet.

She said, "You have laid much groundwork for it, and when you have the foundation on which to build and a vision for the function of a group, the structure will unfold."

I thanked them for the help and said that I felt as though they were right there with me while I was working on it.

"We were," they said in unison.

I don't know how to go about the next part. I've thought about it, but don't have any ideas.

202

"There are two aspects to this next part that you will write about. The first is that learning to consciously create your experience is a process."

How does this relate to the moonpause woman?

"At every stage of our lives, there are both lessons to learn and gifts to give. The moonpause woman has many gifts of wisdom to give to other women and to her community. The social action you just wrote about is one of these gifts. But she also has more learning to do, and becoming the conscious creator of her life is the lesson. The transition to Wise Woman moves a woman into a new way of being in the world and prepares the way for this learning. She has moved through the shadow lessons and is ready to work with the light. She holds within her the opposites of the darkest night and brightest star. She moves from spirit within her into her physical surroundings, recognizing and greeting the spirit in all things. Then she is ready to consciously create. Find the thread which runs through our teachings and see how it might apply to this process."

And the second aspect?

"A song, of course! Weave this thread into a song, a journey song, to be sung on the journey through moonpause into the wisdom and power of the grandmother. When you have finished, come back."

Consciously Creating

Of course, I am having difficulty with the concept of consciously creating my life. This appears to be the lesson plan for the whole next phase of my life which I am just now beginning. Moving through moonpause has initiated me into the building blocks which are the foundation for learning to consciously create. What each of the Grandmothers of the Wind has taught me has led me into a new way of being in the world. Learning to transform shadows into light allows me to move in the darkness of myself without fear. Seeing with Dreamtime vision opens up a whole new world of energy and its movement within me and in the systems around me extending out into the Universe.

Working with energy and ritual allows me to heal myself and perhaps, in time, others. Learning to walk each day in beauty and joy, living in balance with all that is around me, will allow me to develop community where all are respected and honored. Finding the wisdom of my past lives and bringing it into the present gives me a new understanding of myself. Then I will be ready to learn the lesson of consciously creating my life. As I traced this thread of transformation through the teachings of the Grandmothers, a poem emerged:

The Change

Shadow becoming golden light
Petals opening slowly into Dreamtime vision
Scanning and moving the energy flow
Becoming aware of the energy of the Universe
Flowing through our hearts into healing for all.
Beginning to dance our dance in rhythm
With all our relations in beauty and joy
Creating community, honoring the gifts of all
Bringing forward the wisdom of many lifetimes
Learning to consciously create our lives and our world.

I entered the tipi and took my place in the East.
I think I have finished, I said.
Mariah said, "Indeed you have. It has been a long and intense journey from the seeds planted at the Spring Equinox to the fruit now ripe at the Fall Equinox. There are many new seeds within this fruit that will be planted next Spring.

"For now, you will have a time for rest and continuing to work with what you have learned, time to finish within yourself what has been brought to completion on paper. We would like you to continue to journey to meet us once a week. Your work with us has only begun, but we will give you time to integrate the teachings before we go further.

"We like your poem. Each line is a thread from each of our

teachings woven into a beautiful description of the changes which have taken place within you during this time of initiation. We invite you to step out of whatever is left of your old identity and place it in the fire to release it. Your new way of being, the way of the Grandmother, will become more comfortable as the integration process continues."

I could feel myself stepping out of what felt like a set of old clothes, worn thin and full of holes. I placed it in the fire and felt the last remnants of who I was slip away in the smoke.

"Let's sing the journey song you found. This song may continue to grow as you continue your journey."

We joined hands, moving together around the fire and singing:

> Grandmother, Wise Woman, walking in Beauty
> Grandmother, Wise Woman, living with Joy
> Grandmother, Wise Woman, healing the Vision
> Grandmother, Wise Woman, dancing the Dream.
> Grandmother, Wise Woman, Woman of Spirit
> Grandmother, Wise Woman, Woman of Truth
> Grandmother, Wise Woman, Woman Creating
> Grandmother, Wise Woman, Woman of Power.

206

Other Works by Linda Heron Wind

New Moon Rising: Reclaiming the Sacred Rites of Menstruation
(1995)
A book about reclaiming the power of the feminine in our daily
lives.

The Inner Work Tape Series
Part 1: Exploring the Inner World
Part 2: Soul Retrieval
Part 3: Waking Up the Energy Body
Part 4: The Doorway to the Universe
(Each part sold separately; four tapes in each part.)

Grandmothers of the Wind Songs
Songs on tape from *Grandmothers of the Wind: Menopause,*
Wisdom, and Power

Available from:

Heron Press
P.O. Box 382
Fishers, New York 14453-0382
Telephone (716) 924-5620